OLD MOORE'S DREAM BOOK

D0628222

OLD MOORE'S DREAM BOOK

Explodes the myths and mysteries —
reveals the secret messages

W. FOULSHAM & CO. LTD.
London · New York · Toronto · Cape Town · Sydney

W. Foulsham & Company Limited
Yeovil Road, Slough, Berkshire, SL1 4JH

ISBN 0–572–01345–0

Copyright © 1985 Old Moore Publications Ltd.

"Published by arrangement
with Dr Francis Moore's
Old Moore's Almanack
   © W. Foulsham & Co. Ltd."

Printed in Great Britain at
St. Edmundsbury Press,
Bury St. Edmunds

CONTENTS

INTRODUCTION

A great deal of people who buy and read books about dreams are concerned only with the interpretative aspect – eager to discover what is going to happen to them "in the future". They bother little as to *why* they dream, if it is necessary *for* them to dream and most certainly they do not wish to understand the *mechanics* of the dream life.

In this book, these points are explained before there is any attempt to focus attention on the prophetic aspect of dreams. And, *in* showing the phophetic propensities of dreams, an analysis of each dream is given. Although dreams *can*, to a certain degree, forecast the future, they can only do so because they reflect dominant subconscious desires and impressions that are the very essence of the dreamer. Desires to do so-and-so, to accomplish so-and-so are mirrored in the dream life but – because they show the dreamer actually doing what is wished to be done – this is not necessarily a firm, reliable prediction of things to come. It is, however, to the dreamer. What can be visualized can normally (and within reason) be realized.

A dream of a tall dark male lover will not mean that the girl dreamer *will* meet and marry a tall dark man, but it definitely presupposes she is likely to do so because she *subconsciously harbours desires* for a tall, dark man. She may dream of a short, fair man with whom, in her dream state, she has the most terrible time. This will show she has *secret fears* of short, fair men, or has suffered an unfortunate experience with a short, fair man. Her dream will accentuate the fact therefore, that she had better not marry a short, fair man.

Such a dream is a constant or recurring reminder to the dreamer, from the depths of the subconscious *not* to do what the dream presents as being disastrous, unpleasant, abhorrent or frightening. The pleasant, tall-dark-man dream, on the other hand, shows a girl dreamer what she wants to do and what she should do.

If she marries a tall, dark man – then "her dream has come true". In fact – she has made her dream "come true" because she has allowed her subconscious wishes, reflected in her dream-life, to be *realized*.

These bald statements of fact do not pre-suppose, however, that the dream-life is a waste of time and is therefore not worthy of investigation. No dream is a waste of sleeping time. Most dreams have a very strong element of prophecy and prediction but age-old interpretations have never allowed for psychological analysis. Over-emphasis has been laid on the "future-content" of dreams and too little stress laid on the "past-content". A little blending of the "past-content" (reason for the dream) with the "future-content" (what is likely to happen) gives a far more realistic interpretation of the dream-life.

The primitive theory about dreams is that the soul, detached from the body in the dream state, is doing exactly what the dreamer dreams he or she is doing, physically. The classical theory is that the dreamer is in communication with "gods", and this accounts for the Greek and Roman mythological dream which, in its culminative effect, has become almost a part of Greek and Roman history. The physiological theory is that the state of the body dictates the dream – the full bladder gives rise to the dream of urination, the frustrated body causes the nocturnal dream, the indigestion-ridden body causes the dream of physical pain and discomfort.

The psychological (and the most realistic) theory is that the subconscious life lives in the dream state and that dreams are memories and impressions, stored deep in the subconscious, being resurrected for a few seconds or moments while the conscious mind is relaxing.

And this is the modern theory which is now, more or less, far past the theoretical stage and well-into the practical, acceptable stage. It is that stage and that theory upon which this book is based with the added premise that the future *can* be controlled, to a very large degree, by the way in which we accept and act upon our dreams that are most notable in content and most recurrent by nature.

Pre-natal influence is also held, by some psychiatrists, to exert certain controls in our dream life. This theory can only be accepted on the basis that we inherit certain tendencies from our forebears that manifest themselves in our conscious actions and that, due to these character-facets, we dream along the same lines our parents dreamed. But there is no copyright of the dream-state, for indeed, all people dream their own original dreams all of the time for the dream-state is a reflection of life as it is lived by each and everyone of us – by our forebears and by ourselves. But we – living in a modern era – dream more modern dreams than did our predecessors. While our grandparents may have dreamed of nothing more disastrous than a falling apple we, of this day and age, are far more likely to dream of a falling nuclear bomb.

The theory of premonition is acceptable within the psychological theory of dreams because countless numbers of people are gifted with a kind of second sight and this manifests itself in the subconscious mind in the dream-state rather than (or instead of) in waking, conscious state.

Ancient dream interpretations are based on the sciences of Astrology and Numerology, certainly in Mythology. But these old symbolisms will not do for today's sophisticated society. For instance – a certain treatise on dreams reads – "*to dream of an accident at sea means you will be crossed in love*". This is an extraordinarily sweeping statement which completely fails to show the connection between an accident at sea and a lover's quarrel. One might just as well say that to dream of being crossed in love means that one will be involved in an accident at sea! Dreaming of shipwreck would show an obvious *fear* of travelling by sea – or it would be a subconscious fear that one might be *required* to travel at sea, or it might be a definite dream of an experience *of* travelling by sea, being shipwrecked or nearly missing being shipwrecked or merely being *afraid* of being shipwrecked.

The cautious individual, dreaming such a dream, might be determined *never* to travel by sea, especially to cancel his or her passage if a journey by sea had recently been arranged! If the ship (which was to have been the ship to be sailed on) *did* subsequently flounder and sink on that very journey – this would be a prophetic dream and we would have to accept that the dreamer had extra-sensory-perception developed to a degree which manifested itself in the dream-state rather than in the waking-state.

There have been many strange instances of individual prophetic dreams and these are, by and large, very definite instances of the power of the mind to reach out to the future as well as to reach back into the past. This is the psychic theory of dreams and is closely allied to the psychological theory with which we are concerned in this book.

Do not *depend* on dreams to forecast your future – but *do* accept that dreams reflect your character and personality, your subconscious thoughts and impressions, wishes and desires. Accept, also, that your mind *can* reach out into the immediate future and foretell what *might* happen. Accept, too, that as you behave in your daily, conscious state, you "behave" in your nightly, subconscious state . . . that the two are closely-linked, the one interdependent upon the other.

That – in fact – you *can* plan future vitally important moves in career, social and domestic life by the content of your dreams.

CHAPTER 1
THE FIVE FORMS OF DREAMS

We dream when we stand on the threshold of consciousness – when we are about to wake up. We also dream when we are just falling asleep. When we lie down in bed for the night's rest before us – we first of all begin to feel just a little chilly. Cold rivulets of "water" appear to run down our spine – even though the bedroom is warm. This shows oxygen is leaving the brain and our body-temperature is going down.

Thinking, as we are, in that particular state, we begin to have haphazard impressions, though still conscious of the room, of passing traffic, of the ticking of the clock. We are not fully capable of consciously controlling our thoughts and we begin to have silly notions; impressions are jumbled. Many times we wake with a start from this semi-dream-state and perhaps do not go to sleep properly for some time to come. But, generally, this state heralds the approach of proper sleep and we begin to sink further and further *into* sleep.

We may be sure that true slumber is approaching as soon as we feel the slight shivers, as soon as our thoughts start to get jumbled, amusingly incoherent or astonishingly bizarre.

From then on – it is a short step to actual dreaming which takes place as our conscious mind is taken-over by our subconscious mind. Dreams also occur as we approach the waking state – as the conscious mind begins to reassert itself and take over from the subconscious. We may also dream when in deep sleep – but those are the hidden dreams we are rarely able to recall.

Dreams are sometimes triggered-off by the sleeper lying in an uncomfortable or cramped position in bed. The head may be too low on the pillow. Sleeping on one side may not suit the sleeper; sleeping on the back may be causing undue pressure on the spine. Anxiety-thoughts before dropping-off to sleep may cause more blood to continue circulating in the brain than is normal for good, sound sleep. When a person is asleep – one can continue to "hear" sounds such as opening and closing doors, objects dropped on floors, firebells in the streets, children crying. Such sounds resurrect certain subconscious thoughts, memories and impressions (due largely to association of ideas that have something in common with the particular sounds).

"Phosphenes" – those ocular spectra coloured spots in the circulation of the retina, activated by excitation of the optic nerve, are sometimes "seen" in the sleep-state and their fantastic patterns and movements arouse subconscious past impressions that, in turn, give rise to dreams. Again – the light of the moon may be full on the sleeper's face for a period, or a street lamp or flashing sign may impress itself on the somnolent brain.

These experiences of a sensory, auditory and visual nature prompt and promote dreams. Add to these the automatic actions of internal organs – the lungs, the heart, the bladder, the sexual glands – and we have a whole host of mental and physical mechanisms directly responsible for the phenomenon of dreaming.

But don't allow these coldly clinical facts to rob you entirely of your colourful opinions of your dream-life – for there still remains the indisputable fact that dreams are fashioned from character-facets, and character guides and controls the future!

In your dream state you "see" wonderful things, attractive or repellent people – all in glorious colour. Your eyes do not see – of course. They are closed. It is your brain that "sees".

There are five forms of dreams. They are dream *censorship*, dream *content*, dream *imagery*, dream *material* and dream *wishes*.

1. Dream Censorship

This form modifies, or cancels-out, or omits altogether, that which is not desired. Or it regroups memories and impressions in such a way as they appear as the dreamer would wish them to appear, instead of how, in real life, they would appear.

Example

You dream you steal a watch and you get away with it for always. But the actual fact would be that you would steal the watch and be caught. Your dream censors "being caught", disallows this and lets you get away with it.

2. Dream Content

Your experiences in a single dream. First – the "story" of the dream, secondly – the significance behind the story.

Example

You dream you are kissing an attractive girl/man.

Significance – you cannot kiss an attractive girl/man – for you are already married.

You dream you are falling from a great height.
Significance – you are out-of-favour with someone, your wife/
husband, your employer. You "fall" out of favour.

3. Dream Imagery
The sequence of events in a dream. The distracting and unnatural
jumping from one event to the other. The complete distortion and
juxtapositioning of occurrences.
Example
You dream you ride on top of a bus and at once there is a TV set in
the bus and the postman brings you – not a letter – but a new-born
baby.

4. Dream Material
The succession of various events in a dream and the underlying
motif and *motive* behind the events.
Example
You dream you run out of a house, down the garden right into the
sea. A ship sails by and picks you up. But – on board, there is a long
line of chorus girls and a salesman comes up to you and tries to sell
you a new suit. At once the line of girls is a long privet-hedge and
the salesman your father – who died many years ago. You turn to
dive off the ship and the sea is a lush green meadow with a single
tombstone in the centre.
Motif: Great green expanses of sea and grass. Many girls and a
persuasive salesman.
Motive: Vast spaces to which you escape from your house (probably
in which your father died). Forbidden females but your wish to
"dress-up" for them. (The new suit.) The censorship of your father
and the reminder he is dead. (The tombstone.)

5. Dream Wishes
The dream-state fulfilment of a repressed wish or a frustrated desire.
As an adult – the dream is that of a wish that is ungratified in
conscious life, for adulthood lays mature restraint. As a child – the
dream would be that of a fulfilled wish – for children are, as a rule,
un-inhibited, un-frustrated and un-repressed. Maturity has not yet
bred a sense of censorship.

The clairvoyant dream is the dream of premonition with which we
will deal later.
   Dream intrepretation, in its modern, contemporary sense,
devoid of "magical" influences and misleading concepts, is an
analysis of a dream carried out to discover the underlying motives of

the dreamer. The dreamer's dream is interpreted as a picture of the dreamer's attitudes towards life – especially towards his or her individual *future*. It is in the significance of the word "future" that individual, psychological dream-analysis can help the man or the woman towards fulfilling future hopes (reflected in the dream-state), for the dream content is a wishful-thought *for* the future.

Some people dream of immediate occurrences and experiences in daily life. There may have been a happy occasion that day. That very night, the dreamer dreams of precisely that happy occasion. But another person will not dream of that particular happy occasion for many weeks, months, or even years. This is because some subconscious impressions and memories float nearer to the conscious than do others and are, consequently, resurrected much earlier than are those that are buried deep in the subconscious.

Many people dream of childhood experiences when they are well past middle-age – others dream of what happened today.

Dreams sometimes seem to last for hours and hours. One wakes, feeling one has dreamed all night. In fact – dreams are of very short duration but seem to pack hours and hours of experience into a few fleeting seconds.

If a clock, or watch, or bedside ornament were to fall on a sleeping person – the instant moment he was struck by the object could easily form a waking impression of hours and hours of troubled dreaming – culminating in something horrific, like a concrete boulder, the knife of a guillotine, an iron girder falling on the sleeper. The complete dream content (the story) would have taken place in the sleeper's subconscious in the second or so of impact. To dream of being struck by an object when one is actually struck by an object has, of course, no psychic or psychological significance. This is purely a physical experience actuated by the material fact of *being* struck. But – to dream of being hit without any possible material or physical reason is fright with subconscious symbolism

Dreams relieve emotional pressure upon the thinking processes. Dreams condition us to be able to withstand actual shocks when they occur in real life. Dreaming of the death of a beloved one inures the dreamer, in the waking state, against too great a shock – for the experience has already been experienced in the dream-state. To dream of being involved in a car crash conditions the man or woman to withstand the initial, conscious shock of an actual car accident – because the experience has already been experienced.

Few people realize the therapeutic *value* of dreaming. In dreams – we experience horrors we may never have to experience in real life but, if we *are* suddenly assailed by them as physical and mental *facts* – we are innoculated against the first awful impact and therefore stand a better chance of surviving – mentally and physically.

Dreams can *warn* of impending danger, failure, loss of health, for the analytical subconscious, cleared for action in the dream-state and uninfluenced by conscious desires and actions, can present facts in their unbiased state. If the conscious mind insists black is white out of pure obstinacy, knowing all the time that black is black – the subconscious will stand none of this nonsense in the dream-state but will sensibly accept that black *is* black.

Dreams are wish-fulfilments in some cases. Sexual desires, impossible for realization in society – can be "experienced" in dreams and the mind therefore cleared, temporarily, of repressions and frustrations.

Problems can be solved in the dream-state. By morning – all can be as "clear as daylight", because the calm, unaffected subconscious has been able to assimilate and distribute facts without influence from the conscious mind. By morning, the conscious mind is ready and willing to accept the judgement and the opinions of the subconscious – and problems are sorted-out and solved.

Ancient and "popular" books on dream interpretation sought – and seek – to place too many magical properties on the process of dreaming and the influences of dreams. Modern psychological and medical thought places the phenomena of dreaming in correct perspective. It does not, however, decry the prophetic possibilities of dreaming, their penchant for serving as warnings, their propensity for influencing present and future moves for success.

After all – as a person thinks, so he is. As a person *dreams* – so he *wants* to be.

And *can* be.

CHAPTER 2

TYPES OF DREAMS

Diet plays an important part in the building of the dream-world, however materialistic and unromantic that may seem! A heavy dinner or supper shortly before bedtime plays havoc with the digestive tract and is the most prevalent reason for the nightmare. Discomfort in the stomach sends discomforting messages to the brain. In turn, the brain seems to sort out the most horrifying memories and impressions and jumbles these up in such a way as to people the sleeper's dreams with the most bizarre situations. Mercifully, these spasms are of short duration and the sleeper awakens with a jolt. Care should always be exercised in choice of foods before retiring and certainly one should never attempt to go to sleep on a full stomach.

As we learned in the last chapter – a dream that appears to go on for a long time exists, in fact, for a few seconds only. This is like the shutter of a camera being opened for a fraction of a moment according to the time exposure previously decided upon. In those fleeting seconds a whole scene is firmly imprinted on the film inside the camera and when the film is developed the finished photograph can be looked at for many hours.

A dream is released from the subconscious in a matter of seconds and appears to be in view for a long time – but its "life", in time, is little more than the open-shut action of the camera shutter.

But, in the dream-state, time is no longer relative. We can live many hours in so many seconds. Sometimes we hear ourselves shouting "wake me, wake me" – and this nightmarish state of mind appears to endure for long, agonising moments until finally someone *does* awaken us – or we awaken ourselves. The conscious mind always comes to the rescue – though it seems to take an eternity of time in so doing.

Many of us say (with a certain mysterious pride) that we suffer from a recurrent dream that appears to repeat itself night after night. That may be so, but it also may *not* be so. The subconscious is capable of playing so many little tricks on us that we actually dream we are dreaming the same dream when, in actual fact, we have never dreamed that particular dream before. Certain subconscious memories and impressions, similar in atmosphere and event, are resurrected night after night, and this similarity gives us the waking impression that we have "been here before". Indeed, the subconscious mind can play a similar trick on us in the waking state. For instance, when we go into a room or go through a certain sequence of events and have an uncanny feeling that we have been in that room before or that we have done precisely those very same things before. We are apt to treat this very seriously indeed and to consider such recurrent dreams as premonitions of things to come. When experiencing the feeling that we have visited a place or done certain things before we wonder either whether our reason is weakening or whether we are gifted with extrasensory perception and have the ability to see into the future. Disillusioning though it may be these things are normal manifestations of the normal conscious and subconscious minds and have no esoteric significance whatsoever.

At times when we are particularly worried about a certain set of circumstances and dwell on these things a great deal in our working hours, such concentration can cause us to dream of these problems night after night. This particular state is self-created by our having concentrated too much on such anxieties and the recurrence of the subconscious impressions of these things is no more of a phenomenon than is our wilful and continued *thinking* on these things. The recurrent dream, therefore, is not a portent of evil and not a sign of imminent bad (or good) fortune.

A nightmare is a dream with overtones of terror, intense anxiety and perhaps, personal (dreamed) suffering. Let us stress (since this book is intended to help and to assist as well as to intrigue) that the sufferer from constant nightmares is not a person doomed to future misery or danger or death, but is merely an individual with either an upset digestive tract or an over-fevered imagination.

A nightmare is normally Nature's way of releasing hidden, pent-up emotions that, in daily conscious life, find little or no release at all. It is dangerous for an individual to have pent-up feelings, frustrated emotions and repressed reactions to the toils and turmoils of everyday existence. Nature sees to it that the subconscious lives through little moments of terror from time to time in order to innoculate the mind against the onset of very real, and conscious terrors.

If nightmares arise merely from an upset stomach – then this is Nature's way of warning one to be more careful of what one eats and when.

Nightmares usually consist of impressions of falling swiftly through space, of being involved in desperate fights, ascending terrible flights of stairs that go on and on, up and up and up for ever or of being shot or hanged by the neck.

The reason for such dreams is quite simple and shows how well nature is looking after us. Nature knows that the average intelligent and physically healthy human-being has normal dreads and fears of a physical sort. Moreover that the average human-being reads a regular quota of newspaper reports of fights, shootings, violent deaths and so on. In addition, there are horror films, at the cinema and on the T.V. screen, plus a certain amount of fictional reading involving bloodshed, sudden shock and death. This is the average mental consumption of the normal man and woman during the course of a life-time.

Naturally – the mind, steeped in knowledge of all the unpleasant things that *can* happen to the body and to the mind – cultivates an ability to consciously visualize, from time to time, the enormity of such things actually happening. Indeed, it is quite *possible* for all these things *to* happen. One can kill, and dangle at a rope's end. Or be injured or killed in a car crash. Or be shot on a street corner during a hit-and-run fight between thugs and the police. Certainly, on a high building or a mountainside one could lose balance and plunge into a street or ravine below. Or have to mount a high flight of stairs on some mission or the other.

All these things are distinctly *possible*. The more one dwells on them the more horribly feasible do they become. So Nature – in order to soothe the highly imaginative mind – from time to time allows the subconscious mind, in the sleeping state, to "experience" all these calamities. Upon waking, fright soon gives way to reason and a sense of security. The dreadful things have been "experienced". Now – all is well. We can stop imagining what it would be like – *for now we know*.

So the mind becomes calmed, ruffled nerves quietened and thoughts are turned away from horrors and dwell upon more constructive, less frightening things. Finally – they are dismissed. But – should the time ever arrive when we *do* have to experience, in actual fact, some of the terrors – we are better able to cope with them – *for we have experienced them before*.

The therapeutic value of waking from a nightmare is tremendous. For instance, for hours, it might seem, we have been labouring as a prisoner in some dreadful camp. We know that we shall never again be free. Never see the wife or the husband or the children again, or get up and journey to the office or go for holidays in the car. A desperate, dull grey depression descends upon us and life seems completely intolerable. But – in a few seconds – we are awake!

The welcome shafts of light across the ceiling and walls welcome us. There is the clock by the bedside. The half-open doorway leading to the hall. The sound of a train going by in the distance. The immeasurable sense of relief and happiness, the peace of mind and gratitude that descends upon us in those blissful, merciful waking moments is beyond description.

This is great medicine for the mind! Without stirring from our beds – we have been made to suffer the torments of the damned – and glory in the joys of release – all in a few seconds. Now, our minds are better equipped than ever to face up to the normal, insignificant (by comparison) demands of the day. We have suffered and triumphed. The amount of good done to the bloodstream, the heart, the mental processes, is incalculable.

Never curse at bad dreams – nor rail against nightmares.

The waking dream is that dream-state when we are returning to consciousness. Sometimes we associate our normal surroundings with the atmosphere of the dream. If we have dreamed we are talking to a tramp – that tramp seems to project himself actually into our bedroom and is there, at the foot of the bed as we awaken. We continue talking to him for quite a few seconds before our conscious mind takes full command and the subconscious "tramp" fades swiftly out of sight to where he belongs – which is nowhere – of course.

We dream that our bedfellow is getting up and out of bed. With our return to consciousness we see our bedfellow actually rising and putting aside the bedclothes. We say *"Where are you going? Why are you getting out of bed?"* Invariably, the other person is still sound asleep. Then consciousness returns and we feel either a great sense of relief or begin to feel rather foolish.

Dreaming just before falling-off to sleep can be a series of convulsive conscious and subconscious "jerks" – as the subconscious fights to overtake the conscious and the conscious puts up stern resistance. Add to this the physical factor of bodily fatigue and the necessity for sleep plus the lateness of the hour and you have a major human battle.

Healthy, physical fatigue is sometimes defeated by the restless mind that refuses to allow the body to go to sleep. Gradually – the pleasant sensations of approaching sleep vanish – the mind becomes more and more acute – and sleeplessness takes over. There may be an occasional triumph of the subconscious as it succeeds in overtaking the conscious, and wraithy, distorted surface-dreams occur. But the conscious mind wins, the fantasies fade and the body resumes its restlessness. Not until the power of physical fatigue finally takes over does the will bend to the body and the mind-conflict come to an end.

The "falling-off-to-sleep" dream is indecisive, indeterminate and confused. It is compounded of last-minute waking thoughts and subconscious thoughts struggling to get through. It is the easiest dream from which to awaken as the conscious mind is still, up to a point, in control. Once the threshold has been passed – the subconscious rules and real dreams begin.

Daydreams are also a part of the subconscious mechanism but, this time, the conscious mind is not dulled and has not been temporarily robbed of its power. Daydreams are temporary escapes from the vital present. They are usually pleasant vagaries of wishful thinking; conversations between people held in the mind. These dreams are mostly of a positive nature, as the conscious mind commands indulgence only in pleasant thoughts and does not allow the subconscious to intrude with unpleasant thoughts.

The inveterate daydreamer is the person who gets little done, who escapes readily, willingly and often into the little paradise of what might be rather than what could or should be.

The daydreamer is not a man or woman of action. Action by day, and during all conscious hours, does not allow for daydreaming, for jobs have to be tackled physically to be accomplished. Daydreaming is, to the active man and woman, a welcome respite from activity, serves as a rest-period for the body during which it can recharge itself for further effort.

Only when daydreams are allowed to interfere with positive action are they continuously harmful.

CHAPTER 3

THE SEXUAL SIGNIFICANCE OF DREAMS

Many men and women associate dreams with sex and, since sex occupies a perfectly normal and natural part of everyday thought and is, indeed, what makes the world go round (rather than love, which sometimes succeeds in disturbing matters), it follows that sex forms a large part of subconscious memories and impressions. Coupled with this is the fact that sex also occupies a great deal of conscious thought and action. It therefore becomes an inescapable truism that dreams must be peopled with sexual imageries and symbolism from time to time.

Purists who dream a great deal about sexual matters have only themselves to blame. By shutting-out conscious admittance of, and acceptance of, sexual matters they automatically relegate these thoughts to the subconscious, where, in the sleeping state – they will demand resurrection and recognition.

Healthy minded heterosexual people (those who indulge in the normal man-women physical association) do not dream over-much about sexual matters for they lead normal, full lives and such matters are neither frustrated, repressed nor inhibited desires hidden-away deep in the subconscious. They are consciously-exercised thoughts and emotions which have regular physical outlets and therefore have little or no place in the archives of the subconscious.

Frustrated, inhibited men and women sometimes dream of the most outrageous sexual scenes as compensation for their non-sexual activity in conscious life. Once again this illustrates Nature at work – who sees to it the mind is not deranged nor put-off-balance by virtue of inhibition. Here is a safety-valve that enables the dreamer to experience in the dream-state what is denied (wilfully or by circumstance) in the waking-state.

The nocturnal dream of the adolescent boy and girl is due, not to repression or inhibition at that tender age, but more to the mechanics of the body-mind relationship which produces this experience in lieu of actual physical adventures. This is not to be dismayed but rather to be welcomed, for it shows the perfectly normal and healthy girl or boy entering rational puberty.

When adult men and women, married or single, experience noctural dreams of any degree of frequency – this shows an unsatisfactory emotional life if married and a frustrated emotional life if single. This is, however, nothing of which to feel ashamed, for, if conformity or non-conformity, social taboos or religious norms, disallow the individual the right to pursue a normal sex-life, Nature will surely take over and adjust.

There are, however, dreams of a sexual nature that indicate a definite pathological disturbance in the individual. There is, for instance, the male dream of castration. This indicates a wish to be rid of masculinity, possibly a strong desire to be female instead of male. Or, again, it could demonstrate a strong denial or masculinity through fear of getting married, fear of responsibility, fatherhood, and so on.

Feminine dreams of organ-envy of the male show a strong inclination to masculinity, possibly a desire to side-step the inconveniences and fears of pregnancy and motherhood.

Male dreams of associations with fellow-men, and female dreams of associations with fellow-women could indicate homosexual and Lesbian desires – but could equally as well show fears of parenthood, child-making and child-bearing. Such dreams would show desire for sexuality without the attendant and ultimate responsibility. Such dreams show more courage than, for instance, the male castration dream which seeks to deny everything or the female organ-envy dream which seeks to deny motherhood and take-over the more pleasant and less-responsible role of the adult male.

But many dreams of a sexual nature have no other importance than to serve as escape-channels for extravagant sexual wishful-thinking. As such they are harmless and, once again, show Nature coming to the aid of the human.

Dreams of pregnancy and childbirth are very common in the female – from adolescence onwards. Some are dreams of fear, of the actual moments of childbirth. These dreams are best dreamed for they help remove the *ultimate* fear and pave the way towards happily-anticipated childbirth when the right time arrives.

Pregnancy-dreams by spinsters denote their state of life and show presence of a strong, but denied, maternal instinct.

Dreams of hatred towards a new-born child can indicate an un-natural lack of maternal instinct, but this can never be taken for granted – for, once a woman has become a mother, whatever past distaste may have been – Nature usually assets herself and brings to the surface the latent and unsuspected maternal instinct.

Men (especially husbands) who dream they are having a child themselves seek to take the burden from their wives' shoulders. On the other hand – this could be a furtherance of the castration dream in which they try to rationalize their deep-rooted desires to be females themselves.

Male dreams of sexual adventures with girls and women are, basically, primitive in origin and merely demonstrate the sexual nature of man which is, in truth, to be the hunter of women. Only social order and the laws of the church halt the man in his stride, invest him with intelligence and intellect with which he sees the sanity of the laws and obeys them. But that is not to say his basic nature cannot go a-rovin' by night! And it does not make him an unfaithful husband or a rakish bachelor!

Female dreams of sexual adventures with boys and men are also primitive in origin, for woman is the hunted. Only social order and the laws of the church – plus her own, intrinsic sensitivity and ability to raise herself above carnal desire – invest her, in turn, with the intelligence and the intellect to confine herself to one man (if married) and to conduct herself with restraint if still single. With her also, there is no constriction upon her sexual meanderings while asleep!

Many men and women dream they are walking or running down a busy street completely naked. This can either be interpreted as an exhibitionist dream or as a dream of sexual inhibition, according to the circumstances and the psychological make-up of the dreamer, male or female.

The exhibitionist-type male or female will dream this dream as Nature's release for their strong desires to display themselves in public hand-in-hand with their natural restraint from so-doing because of the consequences. It may also demonstrate normal exhibitionist-desires harboured by most normal men and women to display themselves during the course of healthy, permitted love-making.

As a dream of sexual inhibition, it would show in the male an earnest desire to make the sexual conquests of which he seems incapable of making. In the female, it can also show the same but it could also indicate a dread fear or surrender to a male.

If such "exposure" dreams are flavoured with a sense of fear, of horror, of being pursued and caught (or not caught) then this is a dream of fear of sexual surrender, or of sexual conquest, or of strong sexual guilt feelings.

If, however, the dreams are accompanied by feelings of happiness, joy and pleasure at the "exposure" they display a subconscious desire for free expression, a denial of inhibition and an un-repressed outlook on matters sexual.

Dreams contain phallic symbols of which the usual male and female are not normally aware. They may seem rather crude in concept — but psychiatry down the enlightened decades has proved (through psychoanalysis) that these symbols are authentic and so often-repeated by the male and female dreamer as to leave no doubt as to their import.

Male phallic symbols are pens, pencils, cylinders, elongated objects, tall pillars, trees, sticks, skycraper buildings, towers, jets of water and so on.

Female vaginal symbols are locks, open doors, running water-falls, holes, apertures, chinks in doors and so on.

Females dream of their bedroom doors being opened, of their eyes being gouged-out, of objects being forced into their mouths. These are fear-dreams of sexual assault.

Males may dream of tearing holes in things, opening locks with keys, entering into rooms, climbing tall buildings, running-up great flights of stairs. These are wishful-dreams of sexual conquest.

Men and women do not have to be married (happily or unhappily) to avoid having these dreams. They dream these dreams irrespective of their status in life. They dream these dreams because they *are* men and women and, basically and by nature, because they are the conquerors or the conquered, the hunters and the hunted.

It is no slur nor slight upon their natures if they dream of these things, whether the sexual symbolism is flagrantly obvious or only subtly indicated. The only way in which one can judge a man or woman by the sexual content of their dream-life is to say – "here is a lusty, normal man and here is a normal, sexually-aware woman".

So great is the sexual nature of man and woman that, whether denied or fulfilled, the subconscious, from time to time, will people the dream-life with sexual fantasies that reflect both frustration and fulfilment.

Females experience menstruation-symbolism in their dreams by flowing water, floods, streaming hose, flowing rivers. By dreams of open wounds and gushing blood.

Males dream of the female breast by dreaming of mountains and hills, of apples, of curved balconies, of fountains and rising, spiralling springs.

Simple dreams of dancing with a partner, writing letters to a partner, shaking hands, walking, riding, driving in a car with a companion of the opposite sex symbolize wishful thoughts of cohabitation.

The female who dreams she is falling swiftly down a deep ravine – or into a fathomless pit – may fear surrendering herself to a man, may fear the ultimate fall from virginity.

The male who dreams he ascends a steep hill, but is reluctant to reach the top, and has difficulty in doing so, may fear impotence. On the other hand, this dream may symbolize his desire to make a sexual conquest of a certain female (or females in general) attended by an anxiety-complex as to whether he will succeed – or if it is right that he *should* succeed.

The phallic symbol in a male's dream may suddenly turn into a cross or a crucifix. This is the spiritual taboo manifesting itself as a warning against impurity.

The woman may dream she holds a cross or crucifix and suddenly it turns into a snake. This is the wishful-dream that spirituality will not triumph and that she will have her desire. Dreamed in-reverse – it is the Church coming to her rescue just as the serpent (male symbol) is about to strike.

Dreams of a sexual nature begin very early in the child mind of the male and female. It is only when experience and sophistication (or inexperience and frustration) take over that symbolism becomes easily translatable by a trained psychiatrist. Very few laymen and women understand or accept the sexual content or symbolism of their dreams. And it is not really necessary that they should do.

CHAPTER 4

THE PROPHETIC AND TELEPATHIC DREAM

Can dreams foretell what is to come? If the "awake" individual possesses powers of extra sensory-perception or is gifted with second sight or a sixth sense, can a sleeper, in his dream-state, also be possessed of these powers?

The logical answer is – *yes*.

More so the sleeper, and dreamer in fact, for his conscious mind is temporarily unable to control his actions. The mysterious depths of his subconscious with its long history of pre-natal influences, thoughts, memories and impressions passed down from generations before him, plus the memories and impressions of his own life from the moment of birth has a far greater faculty for reaching forward into a future *based on the past and the present* than has the conscious mind.

The conscious mind is pre-occupied with *here* and *now* and is poised to take instant action in order to control the present. The subconscious is more involved with what has happened *before* and the way in which it can control the conscious in *future* moves. This action it is more-equipped to carry out when the individual is asleep and dreaming.

History has recorded scores of notable and amazing cases in which Derby and Grand National winners have been correctly forecast in the dream state. In fact, history records cases where the politics and the military strategy of a nation have been changed by virtue of moves indicated by the subconscious in the dream-state.

It is a psychological axiom of great importance and truth that what can be visualized in the waking, conscious state can be realized by powerful enough personal thought-projection. The mind is a radio transmitting set and the minds of other people are radio-receiving sets. The conscious mind can both broadcast thought and receive thought-waves.

The logical answer is *yes* – I repeat – but further logic must be added by surmising that prophetic dreams are controlled by *what has been* in the life of the individual – and that any prophetic dreams one may have *must* revolve around logical possibilities of things to come within one's particular sphere of experience and knowledge. This means that one cannot dream one will be a famous writer or artist *unless* one has a firm ability to write or to paint and has, in fact, written and painted, profitably or otherwise, at some time or other in one's lifetime. One cannot dream that next year he/she will suddenly be a best-selling novelist if their respective capabilities and abilities are focused on a career as an electronics engineer. Any more than a writer or an artist could predict, by virtue of their dream-life, that next year they would be a well paid electronics engineer.

A man may dream he marries a wealthy heiress and this can come to pass, but only if his state of life, his attitude towards life and his charm and personality, are of a standard and a level that would encourage a wealthy heiress to look upon him in this favourable light. The hard-working and gifted pianist can dream with great certainty that one day he will be a famous concert pianist and this dream can come true. This is visualization projected forward in the dream-state towards ultimate, conscious *realization*.

A mother can dream that her child is to be murdered. The child *is* murdered. This is a strange blending of maternal instinct, the natural blood-tie and an uncanny sense of perception. This sense she would be able to apply to her child because her subconscious would be filled with memories and impressions of her pregnancy, the birth of the child and the up-bringing of the child. She would *not* be able to dream (with prophetic insight) that a *woman-friend's* child would be murdered.

Dreams can forecast how a business-deal will go, how an important interview will turn out and so on, but only because the subconscious is filled with thoughts and experiences, memories and impressions, revolving around the likely circumstances of the deal or the interview. But this is enough to impart to the extra-sensitive and intellectual human being an ability to marshal subconscious thoughts and desires to a fine point of perception whereby the *wished-for* (or feared) outcome *can* come to pass. So we arrive at the premise that prophetic dreams are resultant from purely scientific origin and not through any magical means. Further, this is the spirit in which one should accept them and, indeed, attempt to develop them.

The dream of premonition of impending danger (the dream that contains a warning of trouble ahead) is a phenomena that science has so far failed to prove or disapprove, but that some people *possess* an *uncanny* ability to reach out into the future in the dream-state is without doubt, though this ability must be attuned in some way, however remote, to the circumstances that give rise to the "seeing-into-the-future" dream.

Telepathy is an accepted manifestation of the projection and reception of the human brain in the conscious state. Most certainly it has been proved that two people in the conscious-state (especially long-married husbands and wives) can have telepathic communication with each other, either while together or parted by time and distance.

There is no reason to discount the theory that two such people in the dream-state can also project, the one to the other, a certain dream-content that can cause both of them to dream the same dream at the same time.

Subconscious sleeping thought-waves are just as capable of being broadcast and received between two brains as are conscious waking thoughts. Probably more so, for, in the sleeping-state, two people closely connected with one another are both doing precisely the same thing at the same time – sleeping. And both people are temporarily robbed of consciousness and this lack of conscious thought prevents either partner from doing anything physical or mental that might prove distracting or be a means of diverting thought-projections and beaming them onto other "foreign" wave-lenghts. Both brains are in a comatose state and are therefore readily receptive of telepathic, subconscious communications.

Such a state of "sympathy" can only be present between two people who are deeply in love with each other and who have suffered together, lived together during trial and trouble, joy and gladness; two people, in fact, who have become almost as one. Father and child, mother and child, brother and sister, husband and wife – these are the close relationships that make dream telepathic communication possible and workable.

Between strangers, though they may be strangers in love, the phenomena would not be normally possible as sufficient rapport and affinity would not have been established. The greatest thing is, of course, the blood-tie that exists between blood relatives, but the well-established husband-wife relationship is often enough, depending on length of marriage etc.

If not dreaming precisely the same dream at the same time, a couple so attuned, mentally or physically (or both), can dream on the one hand, the "question" dream and on the other, the "answer" dream. The husband can dream he asks his wife a question and the wife can dream she gives her husband an answer. Comparisons made between the two prove that, at the time the husband dreamed he was asking his wife the particular question she was dreaming she was giving him the particular answer required. And it is interesting to note that the two dreams will have precisely the same point in common.

Many times one hears a person say, quite suddenly – "Oh! you've broken my dream". Up to that point the person has completely forgotten the dream. If it wasn't for a sudden association of ideas the dream would never be resurrected. But a chance remark, a particular "atmosphere", a certain set of circumstances suddenly duplicates the atmosphere or conditions of the forgotten dream and the dream immediately leaps from the subconscious and takes its place in the conscious mind.

Such dreams could have a prophetic content. The dreamer could dream the partner has lost a great deal of money. This dream could be forgotten upon waking. Later in the day, the partner could say – "If I am not very careful, I stand to lose a lot of money on that deal." Immediately the dream is said to be "broken" and the dreamer tells the partner that he or she dreamed the night before that the money *was* lost. The partner can then either dismiss the deal and *not* lose money or he can go ahead and *lose* money when the prophetic dream would have come true. If the partner is wary and succeeds in *not* losing the money – then the dream is said to be a cautionary dream.

The dream within a dream is that dream in which the sleeper deliberately (though unconsciously and effortlessly) turns a dream into the sort of dream he *wants* to dream. This is an extension of the daydream translated in terms of the subconscious nightdream. As consciously the individual may wish a certain bad situation to be good, and daydream that it is after all good, so the sleeper dreams he is dreaming a bad situation to be good. To simplify the foregoing let us say that Mr. B effected a disastrous investment and lost heavily. By day he allows himself the luxury of daydreaming about how good it would be if he had made a good investment and made a lot of money. That night he projects this daydream into his sleeping state and rejects the subconscious awareness of failure interpreted as the dream *of* failure. Instead he dreams he is asleep and is dreaming the more pleasant dream of a successful investment. He does not convince himself (in his dream) that success *is* his. He is aware he is *dreaming* of success but knows nevertheless that all his thought projection (the dream) *is* purely a dream.

He awakens, temporarily refreshed by the experience of having lived through the pleasant circumstances *of* success. This is a trick devised by Nature to allow the worried, perplexed and depressed individual to soothe his fevered brow for a few dream-seconds. After such a dream he is better able to tackle the immediate problem of being not so successful; not, as one might suppose, to feel miserable! Horror-dreams suffuse the awakener with abject relief that horror does not, after all, exist. Success and happiness-dreams inoculate the awakener with extra fortitude with which to face up to reality.

The very essence of dreaming is that it allows for the hidden schizophrenic in all of us to emerge from time to time. Living on the same mental level all the time would be beyond human endurance. The average mind is so filled with fantasy and fictional thought that it is allowed free or full expression in daily conscious life and therefore a second and completely different life is fundamentally necessary in order to preserve sanity.

This second life is surely the dream-life.

The dream-life has to embrace horror, terror, fear, fright and flight. It has also to embrace joy, happiness, success, achievement, triumph. The average conscious life does not necessarily afford an equal share of happiness to the unhappy or an equal ration of unhappiness to the happy. As too much happiness would drive us crazy with boredom so too much unhappiness would drive us to despair. Our dream-life sees to it we subconsciously experience a little of both – to balance our experiences in this present, actual, conscious life.

Even if the dreamer is the type of person who never remembers his dreams, he nevertheless *dreams* and his subconscious mind benefits by the dream sequences experienced and automatically passes this benefit to the conscious mind which reacts accordingly in normal daily life to advantage in future planning.

CHAPTER 5

HEALTH AND THE DREAM-STATE

Most people at middle-age or past middle-age are more pre-occupied with personal health than are younger folk. Young people who allow health to occupy too much of their thinking-time are hypochrondriacs or the unfortunate chronically mentally or physically ill. Anxiety-thoughts in regard to personal health are usually the prerogative of the older man and woman.

Suppressed conscious worries about ill-health usually find an outlet in the dream-state and lead to dreams of operations, prolonged illnesses, and, in some cases, to the "death-wish" dream. If a man or woman is particularly susceptible to suggestion and attaches too much significance to dreams of indisposition then beware, these dreams can project themselves into the conscious, waking-state and can, in fact, create the *symptoms* of the dreamed-of ailments.

Normally, though, the sick anxiety-ridden personality dreams the "reversal dream" – the dream of good health – and awakes refreshed and determined to dismiss negative thoughts of indisposition. This, of course, is yet another indication of the therapeutic value of dreaming.

People who, in the waking-state, are anxious about their sex lives and feel they are over-indulging themselves are likely to dream of pain in the genital areas as a form of "self-punishment" for their excesses. The person who suffers from very real and chronic headaches dream of a miraculous pain-killing drug that banishes pain for ever. Or he might dream the "pain-projection" dream in which he transplants his personal pain into someone else, and is the sympathetic and consoling onlooker. The toothache sufferer can determine, in the dream-state, to shift the pain to another part of his body, and dreams that it is his back or his leg that aches and not his tooth. In the dream he can functionally shift the pain from his tooth so that his brain dictates to his body that the pain is no longer centered in his tooth but in another part of his body. And he will, as he sleeps, feel the pain in the new place.

A man or woman who wishes to avoid a difficult circumstance

of existence will dream of an illness that prevents this circumstance from taking place.

The middle-aged woman, conscious of the onset of her menopause, will dream of her days of youthfulness. The middle-aged man fearing the approach of impotence will dream of youthful vigour and manhood.

Sleep is a voluntary return to the womb from which we came. Sleep is a recurrent "death", differing from actual death only by virtue of the fact that our conscious mind automatically recalls us when the mind and the body have been refreshed, replenished and re-charged.

As we sleep so we demonstrate our attitudes towards life. If we are weak, humble, inferiority-ridden we curl up, our knees towards the chest in the fœtal (in the womb) position. If we show a brave face to the world then we sleep on our backs, limbs stretched out. On one side or the other we turn our backs on adversity and are resourceful and courageous. People who shun the world and seek solace and comfort normally sleep on their stomachs.

People, and especially middle-aged folk, seek escape from life in the sleep and dream-state, especially so if they suffer from ill-health or imagine they do or fear they will. On the other hand many middle-aged people are afraid to fall asleep because they fear the content of their dream-state. These are the men and women who are basically healthy, but who subconsciously worry about ill-health and, in their dream-state, enact all their fears of illness, operations, incapacity and so on. Waking from such dreams, is of course, greatly revitalizing, for the morning invariably brings realization of personal *good* health. This is a type of enforced insomnia, a state of mind that rejects sleep deliberately.

Younger folk sometimes suffer from somnambulism (sleep-walking) – this is the dream turned into action. A boy may hate his father and, in his dream-state, rise from his bed and go into his father's room and stand and stare down at the sleeping form of his father, and in his dream-state, go through the actions of striking him. Satisfied, he will turn round and, still sleeping, return to his bed and continue his night's rest. This is Nature's way of allowing the body to work-off his repressed hatred without actually doing anything about it. This is a merciful escape-route that prevents many a crime from being committed. This is an action that keeps many a man or woman healthy and mentally stable where, otherwise, ill-health and derangement would occur.

People who suffer from bronchitis, asthma, catarrh of the nasal passages and such-like conditions dream of fighting to regain breath, to escape from closed-up rooms and so on. Automatically they awaken and restore their normal breathing and respiratory functions. Seldom do they dream of the actual affliction itself. This is invaribly disguised and takes the form of a fictional, frightening situation from which escape is imperative.

When the heart beats to excess in the dream-state, the dream is usually of speed or a dream of pursuit, of being chased, of escaping in a great hurry. The dream does not make the heart beat faster. The fast-beating heart gives rise to the dream, in the same way that the sensual dream does not activate the nocturnal emission – the emission prompts and designs the dream.

Many old people (and young ones too) who are afflicted by a serious organic disease prolong their own lives by their dream-content which is largely composed of positive, "will-to-live" dreams. A conscious hopelessness in the waking-state is exchanged while asleep for a subconscious hopeful state by way of natural compensation and an illustration of the mind's inherent awareness of the desire for and the necessity of survival.

The death-wish dream is never to be taken seriously. The subconscious mind is aware of the possibility and the inevitability of death almost as soon as it commences to function at birth. It is, indeed, one of the first subconscious desires of the new-born baby's mind, as a wish to return to the comfort and security of the womb from which it has so suddenly been ejected. Superstitious folk attach too much importance to the death-wish dream investing it with completely unnecessary unscientific and totally unfounded significance.

To dream of the wished-for death of another person in the immediate family or social or business circle is, patently, a manifestation of hatred, dislike, antagonism, jealousy or envy directed *towards* that particular person. The dreamer of such a dream need have no fear that he or she is potentially a murderer. Such dreams are merely extensions of a hate-complex which find "realization" in the dream-state. Mercifully so, for conscious, drastic action is halted by the satisfaction of having "experienced" such action or satisfaction in the dream-state.

CHAPTER 6
DREAM INTERPRETATION AND ANALYSIS SECTION

This Interpretation and Analysis Section contains an alphabetical listing of dream "*atmospheres*" rather than dream objects. It is the *theme* of the dream that often contains the possibility of a forecast for the future, based on present and past conditions. With each listed "atmosphere" dream there is a short analysis of probable psychological reasons for the particular "atmosphere".

The "atmosphere" of the dream is the *dominant impression the dreamer gets during the dream-state*. There can be an atmosphere of terror, speed, falling, a primitive atmosphere, an atmosphere of something unidentifiable, of water, of fire, of adventure. Into those atmospheres can come all sorts of objects and all types of images, people. It is not the dreaming of a pen, for example, that holds the predictive feature as much as it is the atmosphere in which the pen appears that is of significance. A tree may be the object of the dream, but the importance lies in the atmosphere in which the tree appears – a stormy day, a sunny day, in a cemetery or in a rose garden, even growing in the middle of a bedroom. Add to this a psychological analysis of a *reason* for the appearance of the tree in that certain place (atmosphere) and one has a practical and up-to-date treatment, far-removed from folklore, legend, myth and magical import.

To complete each dream "atmosphere" – a suggestion for possible future moves is given based on the dream itself and the psychological analysis of the dream "atmosphere".

DREAM ATMOSPHERE	INTERPRETATION
A. Adventure. Discovery, pursuit, voyaging across lands. Strange people, exciting situations, dangerous conditions and you triumph over all.	You seek a way out of a humdrum life, you yearn to find your feet in some other field of daily activity. Hidden talents lie within.
B. Bombardment. Not by bombs in actual fact, perhaps, but by problems, perplexities, people. You are confused and mentally attacked on all sides. There seems to be no escape and you seek to shield yourself but this is unsuccessful.	Your life is too full and confusing. You have not the mental or physical ability to keep up with it all.
C. Children. The air is full of the laughter of little children. Or perhaps *you* are a child again. The cry of a child appals you and you rush here and there in an attempt to find the child.	The retrogressive dream. The escape from adulthood. The maternal and paternal wish unfulfilled. Maturity is too hard to bear.
D. Death. Yours, or that of a loved-one. Or there is fear of death in the air. You look down into an open grave. You read of sudden death.	The dream of the introvert or the hypochrondriac. A fear of future loneliness, of being forsaken. Also the dream of self-pity and inferiority.
E. Explosions. The flare-up of tempers, the rows and arguments. You are in the middle of an explosive scene. Or there is a real explosion. The world collapses in front of your eyes.	You live in anticipation of being continually opposed. Pent-up emotions within you strain to be released and expressed. You feel you have some inner power that can baffle your adversaries.
F. Falling. Through space, down a long flight of stairs. Or you are surrounded by falling objects. There is a feeling of weightlessness. You grab hold of nothing as you fall and you cannot see the end.	You fear committing a "sin". Or making a grave mistake. Or falling out of favour with someone. You have a . responsibility which you fear. Or others are falling away from you and leaving you solitary.
G. Grotesque. Everything is highly-coloured, exaggerated. Faces come and go. People are distorted, ugly. You feel you are in a weird world of improbabilities. You feel you are part of an incomprehensible world of fantasy.	There is a highly-imaginative side to your nature trying to get through. You probably have hidden artistic or creative talents that are submerged into an everyday, conventional existence. These need to be brought out into the open.

PSYCHOLOGICAL ANALYSIS	POSSIBLE FUTURE MOVES
Frustration is your main problem in life. You live only half your mental capacity. You are bound by convention.	You will break away eventually and become an individual in your own right. There are good things ahead, money, possessions.
People make too heavy a demand on you and you regret taking on so much responsibility. But you are afraid to call it a day and to retire from the fray.	A nervous breakdown may show the way out. You will make good use of this and emerge a better person. Responsibility will be yours.
Memories of your childhood occupy too much of your present thoughts. Or you may be frustrated as a parent.	A sudden crisis will shake you out of your regressive spirit. Or you will be forced to take on a very big task. You will succeed in this.
You look backwards too much, and inwards too. Try to look outwards towards others and develop more feelings of self-confidence.	The death of a loved-one will pull you up; you will have to stand on your own feet. This will be the making of you.
Parents or people have kept you down under for too long. Breaking-point is near when you will have to assert yourself once and for all.	A great turn-about in your life is due. There will be a violent change of routine. You are about to become a real individual at last.
A guilt-complex exists in your life over something or someone. Perhaps your religious beliefs are too rigid or too demanding. You are possibly hide-bound by convention.	It is likely you will commit a "sin" at last and all your repressions will clear and life will take on a new, positive meaning, with new friends and associates.
More than likely you are in the wrong job or following a career that is not best suited to your capabilities. You know this but a sense of responsibility holds you back. Try to be adventurous for a change. Dig-up your hidden desires and discover the real you.	You may burst upon the world quite suddenly with a startling creative work. It will not be possible for such as you to be held in check for ever. The near future may be the beginning of a new life, which may well favourably influence your personal income.

35

DREAM ATMOSPHERE	INTERPRETATION
H. Holiness. A church. Candles. Perhaps you are in a confessional. There is organ music and a general feeling of spiritual comfort and solace. Or you are alone on a high place and praying.	You seek spiritual advice or you seek to deny this. Perhaps you do not believe, but wish to. Again, you may wish to run away from life and to seek shelter in religion.
I. Indignance. You are protesting violently with someone, or are involved in a scene whereby you seek to justify yourself. There is a general feeling of conflict.	There is a sense of persecution in your life. You feel people are against you or that circumstances are never in your favour. This may be true or merely a figment of your imagination.
J. Justice. You have to pronounce judgement on someone. You hold sudden authority. People are hanging on to your words. Here is a great feeling of elation. You feel sanctimonious and smug. There is nothing you can do wrong for you are a superior being. You feel a trace of sadism in you as you survey the victims of your authority.	The dream of superiority. You hold ˙ too-high ideals and strive to live up to them too hard. But you are forever in fear of judgement yourself, for underneath your facade of virtue is the suspicion that you are not, after all, as good as you appear to be to others.
K. Killing. The dream of the knife in your hand, the sudden act of violence that results in death. Or there is a scene of carnage before you and blood lust is rife. You try to escape but can only do so by hacking your way through milling crowds — most of whom you are forced to kill.	You have a horror of losing your temper and going too far. You do not trust yourself and know you lack self-control. There is an intellectual deficit in your make-up which tries to hide itself behind bluff and bluster. You must hew-down your intellectual opponents by brain instead of by brawn.
L. Love. (a) A general feeling of affection, rising from normal family feeling to the heights of ecstasy. Or the dream of sexual conquest of your opposite sex, or dreams of a homosexual nature (man or woman).	A normal, natural dream atmosphere common to those who are happily in love, happily loved. Common, also, to those who are frustrated, embittered, unrequited in love. The "love atmosphere" in dreams is one of the most frequent, as love and sex are so closely allied with such intrinsic emotions in the general state of being alive.
(b) The nocturnal dream, common to adolescents and men and women who lead either a restrained or a celibate life.	Purely physical. Nature's physical safety-valve for the body and the mind.

PSYCHOLOGICAL ANALYSIS

This is a dream of a religious person but it is also the dream of an agnostic. Only individual attitudes towards religious beliefs can analyse this particular atmosphere.

Sometimes in your life you have made a serious mistake and this dogs you now and colours all you do. You live too much on your dignity and think that your past still influences your present.

A deep-rooted sense of inferiority manifests itself in a false superiority. To hide this, you hold yourself up as a paragon of virtue and dispense "justice" right and left. Deep down you know you are wrong.

Sometime in your life you have been seriously opposed by those in authority. This has left a scar on your mind. You have exchanged reason for unrational thought. You act on impulse and try to destroy everyone who is opposing you.

All dreams of love, affection, sexual adventures, even of homosexual episodes, arise from the natural urge to love and to be loved. To dream of love with a partner other than the marriage partner is not a sign of moral decadence, a wish to be unfaithful. It is merely an extension of the present, enjoyed and experienced emotions of being in love. To dream, in the single state, of being in love or of having sexual relationships is merely nature recompensing for lack of the real thing. To dream of homosexual adventures is to reveal a disturbance

POSSIBLE FUTURE MOVES

You are the type of person who will, one day, be brought face to face with stark reality and will then have to decide for yourself what spiritual road to follow. You will make the correct choice in the end.

Danger of domestic, social or business failure lies ahead unless you can make a positive move to obliterate the past.

A slip-up in the future is going to unmask you and reveal your true self to others. But you now have a chance to avoid this by ceasing to stand in judgement against others.

Beware of a hasty move that may cost you friends — maybe even your freedom. You may be in too tight a corner one day for escape.

No "love" dreams are scientifically or psychologically possible of prediction. Future moves in this sphere, if suggested, would be improbable, as the sexual and emotional nature of Man is unpredictable in itself.

DREAM ATMOSPHERE	INTERPRETATION
(c) The dream of jealousy, in which one is jealous of another person's love partner.	Illustrates normal but best-avoided emotions that arise in most men and women at some time or the other in their lives.
(d) The dream of spiritual, non-physical love that transcends the sensual side of love.	Mostly the dream of the physically-impotent or the sexually-fearful. This is the wishful-thinking dream in which the dreamer dwells upon the "ideal" love-state in which their sexual inaptitudes would not be discovered and in which they would not have to furnish proof of virility, potence or sexual performance.

M. Melancholy.

A dream of illness in tones of greys and purples. You feel you are crying. A great weight is on your spirit. The sadness is not recognized as any particular sadness, it is just an unaccountable oppression.	You may either have a masochistic nature that finds pleasure in being unhappy; the poetry of melancholia may have appeal for you. Or there is definite sorrow in your life.

N. Nakedness.

You are running naked down a street. No one seems to notice. Or you are naked in a crowd and people are protesting.	A wishful-dream of the inhibited exhibitionist. Or the dream of the prude who cannot face up to the physical side of human relationships. Or this is the dream of insecurity, in which you feel naked to the world and fear its attacks upon you.

O. Occult.

The dream surrounded by mysticism and an air of the occult. Charms and talismans, the signs of the Zodiac predominate. You feel held in the sway of some supernatural powers in which you place great faith but of which you are a little fearful.	You do not place much store by the realistic, material things of life. You prefer to feel you are controlled by the esoteric elements. This is a lack of faith in humanity, lack of faith in prayer. Yours is the dream of spiritual insecurity.

centre in the mind of the dreamer, but this does not necessarily indicate a homosexual nature and should not be taken seriously or regarded with horror. The inherent bi-sexual nature of even the most adjusted individual will sometimes find free expression in the dream-state while, of course, the conscious-state would strongly deny any practice of a perverted nature.

Dreamt by the hesistant, the over-moral and the too-prim. Also by the man or the woman with an over-emphasized interest in and belief of religious concepts and persuasions. Pathologically, a case of self-imposed inhibition as a cover-up for physical weakness or lack of sufficient bravado to be sexually human.

Self-pity is a personal sin against yourself and has repercussions with others. If there is a real burden on your shoulders your melancholy dreams will be dismissed if you discuss the problems with some helpful person.

If you are a martyr to your circumstances, you will be hurt a great deal later. If you have a present problem there is hope for a future solution as dreaming about melancholy times invariably spurs the dreamer to wakeful action.

If you are not exhibitionist by nature, sexually, you are perhaps a "show-off" and throw your weight about. Or you are inferior and wish to attract attention to yourself but cannot. But, you may indeed feel insecure and your dream nudity is your way of asking others to clothe you in moral support.

The genuine sexual exhibitionist never dreams of personal nudity for this is in fact practised. If you do try to call attention to yourself by bizarre means you are due for a fall. If now appears to be insecure, be assured there is hope for the future.

You are not a realist, more an idealist. You seek solace in nebulous entities rather than placing your faith in the practical, material things in life. You lack a solid sheet-anchor in life and will be willing to follow any star if you think it will bring you happiness.

You may make out well with those who share your beliefs, but practical people will discard you if you persist in your esoteric persuasions. Something dynamic in your life will bring you down to earth with a bump!

DREAM ATMOSPHERE	INTERPRETATION

P. Primitive.
The earthy dream, with everything dull and waterless. You strive to provide for yourself against great odds. Perhaps there is a barren plain — empty.

The dream of abandonment. An inability to face up to reality. You prefer the struggle for survival, even though this is hard-going.

Q. Quest.
A long ladder, reaching far up. Or a long narrow pathway and you know you must ascend this. You do not know what is at the top. A dream of an infinity of space forever upwards.

The dream of ambition — of heights to be attained, of fields to be conquered. You have a great deal to do in life but are vaguely perplexed with the enormity of your task. Possibly you are not really quite sure of what you do wish to accomplish — but the nagging insistence is there all of the time.

R. Rushing.
All is rapid movement. A car speeds and crashes. There is a plane overhead that dives straight for you. As it, also, crashes, it bursts into flame but now it is a house on fire. All around you objects and people seem to be going by at incredible speed.

The dream of the neurotic personality. Life seems too short in which to do everything and there is an ever-present fear that this mad rush will bring about a crash, a great calamity, that all your hopes will vanish in flames.

S. Spiritualistic.
You dream you are communicating with the dead. There is no fear and the spirits with whom you speak are gentle and kind.

A fear of death haunts you, though you may be young and healthy, or older and fit. But you seek to disclaim your fear by projecting yourself, in your dreams, into the spirit-life, where you are assured that death is, after all, beautiful and that friends will be waiting to welcome you.

T. Terror.
There is a bursting nuclear bomb or some similar holocaust. In the great mushroom of smoke and flame you see a serpent. Or coiling snakes writhe in flames and you are surrounded by billowing smoke.

The contemporary fear of nuclear war expresses itself with many people — especially those in middle age. The bomb, in the dream, is symbolic of all personal disaster and its appearance in the dream-state is consistent with this day and age. The serpent and the snakes represent sexual guilt, a feeling that one has to atone for one's sins and that holocaust and destruction will be the ultimate end.

PSYCHOLOGICAL ANALYSIS

Perhaps this is a self-imposed task for you dislike a life of ease and those around you who live it. Possibly, though, your intellect will not reach out far enough.

You are over-burdened by high ideals, possibly a plethora of talent that seeks expression. Your ego is over-developed and you are frustrated on all sides.

You are anxiety-ridden and lack control. You could achieve a lot more in life by being a deal calmer. You are not capable of trusting your own judgement and over-assess the speed at which you can get things done.

You have morbid overtones and are introspective. But such a person hangs on to life to the end — and you will defeat the very thing you most fear.

You are victim to today's predominant fear and this is used in your thoughts as the ultimate you can visualize in terror. A dream of snakes alone is a guilt-dream connected with sexual activity but nuclear science allows, now, for even greater feelings of retribution to colour the guilt-complex. Many decades ago — such an enormity of punishment would not have impressed itself so vividly on the subconcious.

POSSIBLE FUTURE MOVES

One day you will have a choice of luxury or hardship. A great deal will depend upon your choice.

Soon — the inevitable must happen. You will achieve some sort of fame. But will it be that which you think you seek? Probably not. But, whatever it is, it will bring its own particular reward that will bring great happiness to you.

There will come a crash, but this will be a mental one. After that — you will readjust and will become a far calmer person able to do all you wish to do with a measured step. Then will come success!

The future will hold good health for you in spite of your fears. So much so, that you will embark on a great new adventure in life.

Your guilt-comlex will one day be "exploded" and revealed to be more a thing of the mind than an actual physical lapse. As to destruction by a nuclear bomb — this is in the lap of the gods and is no one's — or everyone's — inevitable destiny. You, personally, will live to be a source of inspiration to others.

DREAM ATMOSPHERE	INTERPRETATION

U. Unidentifiable.

Vague faces, indeterminate places. You have been here before, you feel but cannot quite place anything. This dream has been dreamt before — these people seem so very familiar. There is the landscape we have never visited — but we seem so familiar with it. And someone speaks — says a certain thing to which we know the response — but we stammer and stutter. The right thing to say will not come.

The dream of the hesitant, indecisive personality. In life — you feel sure you know all the answers — but faced with the questions you are totally tongue-tied. You are an armchair-traveller — relying more on dreams than on reality to carry you happily through life.

V. Victory.

You dream of personal triumph over great odds. Everything you handle is successful. People on all sides are lauding you and singing your praises. You career through your dream on a landslide of achievement.

The dream of the compulsive success. The dream that projects success into waking hours.

W. Water.

You are drowning — or a rush of water is fast approaching you. Perhaps you are in the depths of an ocean — struglling to rise to the surface. Or you are directing streams of water into a vast infinity of space.

Many such dreams are associated with and triggered-off by the desire to urinate and such dreams succeed in awakening the sleeper. Otherwise — to dream of water in the circumstances described shows you flooded-out by your own impetuosity and carefree outlook on life. But you fear that one day this attitude will defeat you and that you will be submerged in the negative chaos of your own confusion.

X. The Unknown Quantity.

The confused dream, in which nothing is clear, all is chaos and waking thoughts on the dream cause turmoil in the conscious mind. The dream that "develops" so many photographs from subconscious impressions and memories as to make the dream-content vague, disturbing and hardly remembered at all.

Confused conscious thought gives rise to this dream-state, a state that is very prevalent among heavy sleepers and those who have the ability to drop-off to sleep almost as soon as their heads touch the pillows.

Y. Youth.

A dream of young boys and girls. Perhaps yourself when young. Of lovers kissing. But, over all hangs sadness, for a coffin in the background shows that they are not long for the world, or that

The middle-aged dream of despair that youth and the capacity to love as the young love has gone forever. When there is no coffin — the dream belongs to youth itself and is a projection of youth itself. But the coffin denotes the

PSYCHOLOGICAL ANALYSIS

You are an inveterate wishful-thinker. You do not do things, rather are you content to just think about doing them. Because of this — you get the impression you have met people before, visited certain places, done certain things. It is easier to daydream than to *do*. And so brilliant are your imaginings — you succeed in convincing yourself that things are what they are not.

A high rate of intelligence may get the better of you and you are fast becoming a far too superior being. This makes you walk over others to achieve your own ends.

You have a grasshopper mind that enthuses on this, that and the other all at the same time. You find it hard to be negative about anything and can create great enthusiasm within yourself and with others for various ideas and projects that, at best, are nebulous and built on weak foundations.

Dream-state of the mainly un-intellectual whose days are occupied more in manual labour than in brain work.

The dream dreamed by the young is just a natural dream of prevalent desires to be fulfilled, but the dream dreamed by the older man and woman is the dream of resignation to the inevitable passing of time.

POSSIBLE FUTURE MOVES

Tricks of the mind and the memory will trip you up one day. This will lead to a lot of misunderstanding but out of chaos will come circumstances greatly in your favour!

Later life may bring a sudden failing in intelligence. You burn up too much brain power in too short a time. But there will be ample compensations.

Move less rashly. Think before you speak and act. Do not overwhelm others with your enthusiasm. The day will come when you will run past yourself and the consequences may well be dire. Look to good friends, now, to pull you up in your impetuosity, and there may well be a chance for you to land on your feet in the near future.

No predictive possibilities.

No predictive values.

DREAM ATMOSPHERE	INTERPRETATION
here, in the coffin, is your *own* lost youth.	disappointments and the frustrations of age.
Z. Zoological. You dream of being surrounded by all types of animals, or there is one animal, a composite of many animals, at once frightening and menacing. Or the dream is that of being attacked by an animal, or hunted down by a pack of fiendish creatures whose shape and form you cannot recognize.	The dream of the unknown "terror" element in a person's life. The characters in the dream take on the appearances of animals because the dreamer disallows his imagined enemies to be real people yet is ready and willing to think of them in terms of individuals with animalistic ideas and attitudes.

The typical "atmospheres" re-created in the Tables you have just read are a cross-section of dream-states which were noted after examining many men and women and enquiring after the nature of their dreams. Most people who were questioned agreed that a dream had more of a "theme" or an "atmosphere" than it had a specific beginning, middle and ending and very many men and women of the same type of personality appeared to experience similar dream "atmospheres", consistent with their particular type, character and personality.

Dreaming about objects, as we have stated, is no indication of dream-content. It is the circumstances surrounding the dream of a specific object that holds the key to the dream-content and which permits interpretation and analysis together with a broad outline of the person's character upon which to base possibilities of future events to come, within their particular framework.

Seldom do people dream "out-of-character" with themselves. That is to say, they dream within the confines of their character-facets, within the circumference of their personal experiences in life, within the scope of the subconscious impressions they have had and the memories they have stored. Neither will they dream beyond the realms of possibilities encompassed by their particular type of person. An interpretation of their dream-content, taken over a long period, is therefore a pretty reliable indication of true character. Character can and does, of course, presage the future for the individual, therefore the dream formulated from the character content of the individual can, without any doubt, contain predictive qualities of things to come within the individual's range.

PSYCHOLOGICAL ANALYSIS	POSSIBLE FUTURE MOVES
The persecution-complex dream. The dream of the person who will not acknowledge people as people but prefers to identify them with animals with whom he compares them. The dream, also, of the animal-hater. Such a person is lonely and embittered and, when cornered by life's problems cowers away in a corner and shows no fight whatsoever.	Dullness ahead, many enemies made, many fights to be fought. View life in correct perspective, and you may realize, sooner than you think, that the world is not all against you!

The mind never sleeps of itself. The body mercifully allows physical fatigue to pull down a curtain on our conscious mind and allows the subconscious mind to take over at regular intervals. This can also happen during the course of a normal day when, and if, the opportunity offers itself.

People who are experts at a specialist job in life sometimes have the ability to project their occupation into their dream-state and this assists in solving their problems, for the sub-conscious mind takes hold of the problem and sorts it out during the hours of sleep. When the sleeper awakens the subconscious automatically conveys the solution to the conscious and the physical man (or woman) acts according to these dictates of reason.

Many people who are required to learn something, such as actors and actresses or learner-drivers who have to learn the Highway Code, commit the lines of the play or the questions and answers of the Code to memory (the sub-conscious) before they drop off to sleep. The subconscious (the human computer) marshals the facts into order while the student sleeps. Upon awakening, the lines fall into place and the questions and answers are easily remembered. This is an irrefutable law of Nature which when fully accepted, appreciated and applied, rarely fails.

Sleep affects our standards and levels of experience, and these various levels of experience, in turn, account for the fact that many dreams appear to be completely nonsensical. One dreams a little from one level of experience (what has gone before), a little more from a second level and still more from another level. All levels grow confused but create the atmosphere of the dream that holds the various levels together in some semblance of coherency.

Dreams do not acknowledge a sense of time. *Now*, in the dream, can be yesterday or tomorrow. *Tomorrow* can be last year, or ten years hence. Neither do dreams acknowledge the single or the plural. "I" can be three people all at once, or three or more people can merge into the one person "I" or "Me".

Love and fear are the two dominant emotions experienced in the dream-state and understandably so as love and fear are the two greatest of human emotions.

In fact, they are the only two emotions, *in* the human breast, from which spring all other emotions and feelings. *Love* creates within itself humour, joy, happiness, exaltation. *Fear* nurtures envy, hatred, greed, maliciousness. In dreams, these two emotions, with their off-shoots, become entangled and emeshed with each other, so that we can dream we hate a loved-one and love someone we hate.

We can dream in "opposites" which represents a type of wish-fulfilment.

The hungry man dreams he is well-fed

The poor man dreams he is rich

The unrequited lover dreams he is fulfilled

The blind man dreams he sees the whole world

The dumb man dreams he speaks to nations

The deaf man dreams he hears all the music in the world

The sick man dreams he is fit and healthy, the cripple that he walks

Dreams have no gender. The girl can dream the dreams of the man and the man those of the girl. But the girl's "masculine" dreams will be coloured and influenced by her femininity, and the man's "feminine" dreams will be coloured by his masculinity. Such dreams could be wish-fulfilments on the girl's part to be a man, and similarly on the man's part to be a girl. Such dreams are transvestite dreams and, if recurrent and forceful, display deep pathological disturbances. Or, if the dreamer of such dreams is completely clear psychologically then the "reverse" dreams are dreams borne of latent (and natural) bi-sexuality and indicate that the vital age of puberty, the changeover from bi-sexuality to heterosexuality (or homosexuality), did not show a complete and decisive *mental* change-over.

Dreams keep pace with existence. Our forebears would never have dreamed of the things of which *we* dream today! But then, of course, they did not have the experiences we have today. And . . . in hundreds of years — men and women will be dreaming dreams far beyond *our* wildest imagination and limitations.

CHAPTER 7
THE BRAIN AND THE MIND

To fully understand the mechanics of dreaming and to be able to separate the esoteric significance of dreaming from the practical phenomenon, you should finally understand the difference between brain and mind.

People do not have "good" brains or "bad" minds in that they apply the natural working of the brain to good or to evil purposes.

They are either brilliant or they are dullards. If they are brilliant their dream-lives are peopled with the thoughts and the fancies that are natural emanations of that in which they are particularly brilliant. If they are dullards their dream-life is so submerged that they are probably not aware they *dream* at all.

The brain is the physical mass of living cells from which thoughts emanate. Some people think more than others and therefore bring more braincells into action. Their subconscious receives more impressions and stores more memories and they dream more. Other people think very little and, as a result, certain braincells become atrophied through not being used. Their subconscious minds store less memories and receive few impressions. Their dream life is consequently less exciting which creates less of an impression and their dreams are therefore not well remembered.

Thoughts are radio waves emanating from the physical brain and are picked up by other people, either in telepathic communication or in direct knowledgeable association, or they are the radio waves projected and received in the telepathic dream-state. The brain is the radio (transmitting and receiving) station which can be tuned into either the waking or the sleeping wave-length — the conscious and the subconscious wave-lengths.

Your brain consists of from 500,000,000 to 2,000,000,000 tiny cells filled with matter called "plasm", a Greek word meaning a mould; highly sensitive matter composed of countless atoms like photographic plates.

It is a perfectly installed system of nerve-wires, complete with switchboard and exchange.

Brain is the organ of mind. Provided there is no apparent physical injury to the brain, the mind can be directed and controlled by the individual. Mind is the personal radar unit by which we detect danger and opposition, send warnings to our body of defensive action that should be taken in order to avert disaster.

Thoughts are many and varied. Circumstances giving rise to these thoughts are equally as varied. Prominent among them are thoughts concerned with the law of self-preservation.

Almost every emanation from the mind has in it some quality that strives to promote this desire to live and to keep on living.

The mind photographs life and retains a permanent positive in the mental retina, the plate behind the sensitive lens of individual observation. Until death closes the shutter, these photographs can be used time and time again. Your mind is an album of impressions, good and bad.

Thought is mind illustrated, action is the demonstration of thought. Brain houses the thousand and one cells from which come these thoughts, receives and sifts messages of flight, fright, fear, anticipation, joy, sorrow, elation, surprise, the full gamut of human emotions. Emotion is the colouring given to thought. All is a vast intricate circle, vicious by no means until and unless you make it so yourself.

With our conscious minds we carry out our daily actions. We speak, move, eat, drink and remain merry. With our subconscious minds we are apt to deflect our actions from the forward path, to speak falsely, move rashly, create chaos, eat and drink unwisely and become melancholy because we allow past mistakes, failures and errors to effect and affect our conscious moves. With our subconscious minds we also dream. ·

Over half the troubles of individual existence embracing illness, worry, depression and frustration are the direct result of lack of knowledge of the part the subconscious plays in the lives of us all. Too little attention is focused upon positive conscious effort. Yesterday's shadows are allowed to cast their gloom upon the sunlight of today . . . and also influence our dreams at night.

Thinking is a process in which our brain cells are brought into action. All sense impressions of past years are stored up in the billions of tiny cells of the brain. Memories of sound, sight, taste, touch, smell, with all experiences, are preserved even to the infinitesimal details. All that is felt, perceived, thought, willed, from the first awakening of consciousness, survives in cells beyond count.

Millions of little photographs filed away. And vastly numerous are the forgotten pictures of infantile and youthful fears and inhibitions — forgotten, maybe, but not eradicated, neither will they be so as long as the brain functions. This constitutes the subconscious mind.

The outer layer of the brain is made up of numberless cells. These cells look like trees in a forest. The branches of these cells stretch out like branches of trees; they reach out to neighbouring branches, thus making contact. There can be no connected thinking or association of ideas unless, and until, such contact takes place.

And there can be no dream process either — as the dream-state depends entirely upon the correct functioning of the conscious, waking-state.

CONCLUSION

We dream to preserve our sanity. If we did not dream we would become insane. People who say they "never dream" are labouring under a delusion. They are merely those who do not recall their dreams, that's all.

Freud, Jung, Adler and many other time-honoured psychologists and psychiatrists have made their contributions to the theories of why we dream, how and when we dream. And many other authors, lecturers, neurologists, psychologists and psychiatrists have written on dream-interpretation.

Libraries are full of "dream-books" written by the Ancients and translated into modern idiom. Greek and Roman mythology is based largely upon the dream-life and many, many passages in the Old and the New Testament are compiled largely from the daydreams of the writers and also from their actual dreams at night.

The whole world lives a great proportion of its life in the dream-state. In fact, every man, woman and child on the face of the earth lives and leads two completely separate and segregated lives — the waking (conscious) life and the sleeping (subconscious) life. These two lives mix and intermingle, the one influencing the other. Neither life would be whole and entire without the other. Each life is a reflecion of the other.

The conscious, dominant life is influenced by the subconscious life. The subconscious also seeks to dominate the conscious life in its waking-state, for the subconscious can also influence our waking thoughts, words, deeds and actions by resurrecting memories and impressions of past failures and mistakes. If the subconscious is allowed to overdominate, the conscious mind dictates failure to conscious moves based on subconscious domination.

But the subconscious also works as a warning-agent in times of danger, resurrecting past impressions and memories of mistakes made, of warnings heeded, of instant actions taken to avoid disaster. These are the positive promptings of the subconscious and should be obeyed. The negative suggestions of the subconscious are those that sow seeds of unnecessary fear, fear of personal failure, fear of making the same silly mistake once again. These are the suggestions that should be dismissed.

This book has dealt scientifically with dream-mechanism and

has allowed for the predictive possibilities of the dream-life on the premise of the character formulating the dream and the dream, after analysis, indicating the possible path that should be taken, in the future, *by* the particular character.

Only the definitely prophetic dream or the warning dream as dreamed by the specially-gifted individuals can safely be said to truthfully predict a definite event. These events are usually of a tragic or a serious nature, for the violent conflicts in the mind of persons so gifted normally only reach out into the future as a means of giving warning of oncoming danger.

Seldom does such extra-sensory perception espy pleasures to come, and this justifiably and reasonably so, for the gift of extra-sensory perception surely is a gift to be used for the betterment of humanity, to warn it of danger rather than to acquaint it of the happier side of future existence.

Happiness and security can be physically enjoyed and sought-out by normal progress and perception. Danger and death, on the other hand, lurk round the dark corners of existence and are most often sudden apart from being unsought.

Those who dream of dread events and are instrumental in warning others in time to avoid personal or national catastrophies are valuable people indeed. Those who seek to create ultimate disillusionment in the human breast by virtue of self-made claims to predict the future through dreams perform a disservice to humanity.

Those, however, who relate their dreams, and the dreams of others to logical character-facets, and who analyse these characteristics in the light of commonsense, and base suggestions for future moves upon their findings, approach the mysteries of the dream-life in a logical and sound manner.

OLD MOORE'S DREAM
INTERPRETATIONS
WHEN YOU DREAM

From time immemorial dreams and their meanings have been regarded with an interest which places them above mere superstition. Far from being looked upon as idle fancies of the imagination, they have been studied for thousands of years by the Philosophers and Scientists of old and the Psychologists and Professors of our present modern age. Much has been discovered and indeed a great contribution has been made towards a better understanding of the working of the human conscious and subconscious mind.

Everyone has experienced some remarkable and vivid dreams that have come true. Some have been pleasant and some have been unpleasant and everyone who has a cat or a dog has seen them when sleeping quiver, twitch or whimper and make crying sounds as they dream their own dreams just like humans.

To human beings, however, some dreams make so vivid an impression on the mind that they are remembered in detail when awaking, and it is these dreams that one should try to interpret to find out their meaning.

The more you study dreams the more truth you will find in their interpretation. Sometimes one dreams all kinds of nonsense which is quickly forgotten. It is the striking and vivid dreams that are important and portend something about to happen in the life of the dreamer.

It is the dreams that are straightforward that should be regarded as being direct messages. These dreams are the fulfilment of wishes beneath our conscious state, and these wishes show what we most desire to attain when we wake.

The belief of dreams is age-old. However far we go back in history we find dreams were treated as direct messages from divine beings and thus held in great respect. There is no doubt, therefore, of the importance of dreams in the history of the world, and that many dreams and visions have been events casting their shadow before them.

Innumerable instances have been given of warnings told in dreams. In some cases these have been explained scientifically by telepathy or thought-transference.

Explanations differ of dreams showing a knowledge of the future, but it is clearly proved that the inner mind possesses extraordinary powers that forewarn of the good things and the bad things in life.

Fortunes have been made in the field of speculation by the fore knowledge gained during a person's dream.

ABANDON.—To dream that you abandon a person, is unfavourable; it intimates you will lose friendships and favours which it will be very difficult to recover.—To dream that you are abandoned, denotes coming trouble.

ABBEY.—This denotes future comfort, peace of mind, freedom from anxiety.

ABHOR.—To dream you are abhorred, not liked, and if you are troubled at the same, some enemies will injure you; if in your dream you are not troubled thereby, but rather defiant, it is a sign that you will surmount all opposition, and triumph over all your foes.

ABJECT.—Dreaming that you are in a forlorn and abject state, I fear, indicates coming poverty; if, in your dream, you appear cheerful under it, it will only be for a season and prosperity will succeed.

ABROAD.—To dream of being abroad, in a foreign country, denotes a change in your situation in life; you are likely to be unsettled in life, and to change your locality.

ABSENT FRIENDS.—To dream of absent friends but that they are ill, indicates news of a disagreeable nature; to dream that they are well denotes they are in a prosperous state, and that their friendship to you is remembered; to dream of the death of some absent friend foretells good news relating to a wedding.

ABSTAIN.—To dream that you are a total abstainer, denotes good health, success in life; great prosperity.

ABUNDANCE.—Dreaming of abundance denotes success in your plans, and a pleasing life in consequence.

ABUSE.—To dream that someone is abusing you is a sure sign that you will quarrel with the one you love, or your friend, and that someone has been speaking ill of you. In trade it indicates loss and often a robbery, therefore take care of your money. It would be as well also to be careful of your fires and lights, as it often indicates loss of life and property by fire.

ABYSS.—Trouble is coming. You will be in trouble and difficulties from which it will be difficult for your friends to extricate you.

ACCIDENT.—Dreaming that you meet with an accident and injure any part of your body, denotes coming personal affliction, from which you will recover.

ACHE.—To dream that you have aches and pains denotes temporary illness, and some slight troubles.

ACORNS.—When you dream of acorns, it is a good sign; it betokens health, strength, and worldly abundance; if single, you are likely to marry well, and have a numerous family. To a married woman it denotes the birth of twins. To business men it is the omen of prosperity and wealth; and to all it is a good sign. To those in love it denotes success and happiness. To those in difficulties, a speedy recovery.

ACQUAINTANCE.—To dream of an acquaintance, denotes his or their continued friendship. It is a sign that they are sincere.

ACQUIT.—To dream that you are charged with an offence before a court, and acquitted for want of evidence, is a sure sign of the utter confusion of your enemies, and of your own prosperity and stability.

ADMIRE.— To dream that you admire a person is an omen that your partner loves you, without ostentation; and if single, that the one you love is sincere. To dream that you are admired betokens numerous friends.

ADULTERY.—Dreaming of being tempted to commit this crime, and of a successful resistance of it, intimates that in future life virtue will be your guide, that you will prosper, and that your schemes and plans will succeed. But if you dream of being guilty of the vice, it is a sad omen of approaching troubles, and that your prospects in love will be blasted.

ADVERSARY.—To dream you meet with an adversary, denotes that you will overcome some obstacle to your happiness; it denotes that your affairs will prosper, though you have enemies. If seeking a job you will meet with impediments, yet you will overcome them.

ADVERSITY.—To dream of being in adverse circumstances is always a favourable dream; it generally indicates the reverse—prosperity.

ADVICE.—To dream that you are receiving advice, denote difficulties; but you will have wise and faithful friends to help you. To dream that you are giving advice, is a sign that you will be highly esteemed by your friends and acquaintances.

ADVOCATE.—To dream that you are an advocate, or that you are advocating the cause of someone, is a sign that your future position will be a prominent one, which will crown you with high honour, and gain you universal respect.

AFFLICTION.—It denotes a change of residence; to the young and single early marriage, but not agreeable. It is not a good omen. It indicates trouble.

AFFRONT.—To dream that you are affronted by a person denotes disappointment in love, and trouble and annoyance through one that owes you money; in every case you will find it the forerunner of annoyance and discontent.

AFRAID.—This is a dream of contradiction. It denotes that in future trials you will be valiant, and not afraid. That your cause will succeed. That the one you love will prove true.

AGE.—A dream about your age betokens illness.

ALIEN.—To dream that you are an alien, or alienated, is a dream of contradiction—the reverse will take place; abiding friendship and love.

ALLIGATOR.—This denotes a sly, crafty enemy; and such a dream should excite caution.

ALMONDS.—To dream of eating sweet almonds indicates future enjoyment, probably by travel in a distant country. If you relish the almonds, every undertaking will be prosperous; if the taste is bitter, your enterprise will fail; and the expenses of it will be costly.

ALTAR.—To dream you are at the altar, and receiving the holy sacrament, is a very unfavourable omen, denoting severe afflictions. If you are in love, your lover will leave you. If in business, you will suffer losses.

ANGELS.—This is a pleasing and favourable dream. It is a sign of high enjoyment. If you dream you are with them, it indicates that you will have agreeable friends; that you will have prosperity, peace, and happiness. To a married woman it denotes she will have a numerous family; if she dreams of two angels, she will have twins the next birth. It is a happy omen to those in love; their marriage will be aggreable, and they will be surrounded with friends.

ANGER.—To dream you are angry with some person, it is a sign that that person is your best friend. Should you dream that the one you love is angry with you be assured they love you sincerely and will make you happy.

ANGLING.—This dream betokens much affliction and trouble in your life engagements. I fear, too, it indicates sophistry, and the desire to entangle people in your meshes. Do not be guilty of such conduct in any way whatsoever.

ANNOY.—To dream that you are annoyed denotes that you have enemies about you.

APPAREL.—To dream that you have good rich apparel, is a dream of contradiction, indicating want and great scarcity of clothes. If you dream you have no clothes it is also a dream of contradiction; you will have a sufficiency, if not more, of temporal things, and many changes of clothing.

APPLES.—This is a very good dream; it indicates a long and happy life, success in business and in love. For a woman with child to dream of apples denotes that she will have a son who will be very great and wealthy. A good dream for speculation.

ARROW.—To dream that an arrow is shot at you, and that it penetrates your body, is a bad omen. Some person or persons are scheming against you.

ASCEND.—To dream that you ascend a hill, and reach the top, denotes that you will conquer your difficulties.

ASS.—This denotes that whatever troubles or misfortunes at present afflict you, will, by patience and humility, have a happy termination. For a young woman to dream of an ass implies that her future husband will be contented and happy, but not rich, rather headstrong, and determined to have his own way.

ASYLUM.—To dream that you are in an asylum denotes coming personal affliction. But to dream that you are merely inspecting an asylum, denotes that you will be in circumstances that will enable you to help the distressed.

AUTOMOBILE.—To dream you are driving a car is a sign of poverty; if the vehicle is your own it foretells advancement. To dream of riding in a car portends loss of job. If you dream a loaded car comes to your door it foretells that someone will befriend you who will do you a lot of good.

BABY.—To dream that you are nursing a baby denotes sorrow and misfortune, and disappointment in love. For a young woman to dream of having a baby, implies that she is in danger of temptation, and that she will be forsaken by the one she loves, and for a young man to dream that he is married, and is nursing a baby, denotes disappointment in the object of his affection.

BACHELOR.—Dreaming of a young bachelor portends that you will shortly meet with a lover, or friend. But to dream that you converse with an old bachelor is a sign that you are likely to die an old maid.

BACON.—To dream of eating bacon portends sorrow. To dream of buying it foretells that you will quarrel with the one you love and part for ever. It predicts great trials by sickness.

BADGER.—If you dream of this animal, it is favourable. It indicates long life and great prosperity, that you will acquire wealth by your industry, and that you will have to travel much in your own and foreign countries.

BAKING.—To dream of baking bread, denotes sorrow. To dream of baking pies, tarts, &c., denotes that you are to assist at a wedding, or you will be called upon to be married yourself very soon.

BALL.—If you dream that you see persons dancing, and that you are engaged yourself, it signifies joy, recreations, and good fellowship. It denotes the reception of a large sum of money. In matters of love, it foretells happiness and success, and that you will have a large family of boys and girls.

BALD.—To dream of baldness portends approaching illness. For a young woman to dream that her lover is bald, foretells that he will not marry her. To dream that she is bald herself, implies she will be an old maid.

BANKRUPT.—To dream of insolvency is a dream of warning, lest you should undertake something discreditable and injurious to yourself, and opposed by your friends. Therefore be cautious in your transactions and conduct, do not enter into hasty contracts, either in business or love, but seek the advice of your friends, for a step imprudently taken may spoil your future life.

BATS.—To dream of seeing a bat flying in the air signifies that you have an enemy. If it appears flying by daylight you need not fear, but if by night, you are in danger. For a young person in love to dream of a bat denotes that you will have a dangerous rival to annoy you.

BATHING.—If you dream that you are bathing, and that the water is clear and transparent, prosperity and success in business, and in love, will be yours; but if the water be dirty and muddy it is a sign of misfortune, sorrow, and poor health.

BATTLE.—To dream of being in a battle implies disagreement of a serious nature with neighbours or friends, or with the one you love. For a married person to dream of a battle, denotes future difficulty in obtaining earthly goods. But if you overcome in battle, it indicates that you will baffle all the attempts of your enemies to injure you, and that success in business will be yours. In love-affairs your wishes will be realized.

BEANS.—To dream of beans is unfortunate. If you dream of eating them it foretells illness. If you dream of seeing them growing, it foretells contention with those you love best.

BEAR.—To dream of seeing a bear, expect trouble, and that some enemy will injure you; and that if you travel, you will meet with hardships, but the end of your journey will be safely accomplished, and the object achieved. To dream that you are fighting with a bear, and kill it, is a favourable sign of your overcoming a foe.

BEAUTY.—To dream that you are beautiful, is a dream of contradiction denoting that sickness may debilitate your strength. To dream of any friend as beautiful, denotes their sickness.

BED.—To dream of being in bed signifies a very early marriage; and to dream of making a bed indicates a change of residence, and that you will live away from home a long time. To dream of sitting upon a young girl's bedside is certainly a sign of marriage.

BEEF.—To dream of eating beef indicates that you will always live in plenty, though you may not be rich; but to dream of beef, and that you have not the power to eat it, denotes that you will be dependent on another's bounty.

BELLS.—To dream of hearing the bells ring is a fortunate sign. It is a sign of coming good news. To the young it foretells a happy and early marriage to the person so ardently loved by them. To persons in business it denotes the acquirement of a fortune. It foretells advancement in your trade or profession.

BILLIARDS.—If you dream that you are playing at billiards, it indicates that you will be placed in a difficult position, from which it will be hard to extricate yourself. If you are courting a young lady, it denotes that you will opposed by her parents or friends.

BIRDS.—For a wealthy person to dream of birds flying, is very unlucky, it denotes a sad reverse in their circumstances. But for poor persons to dream of birds it denotes a change for the better, especially if they hear the birds singing. If the birds have a beautiful plumage, and are not frightened of you, it indicates elevation to rank and influence.

BIRD'S NEST.—To dream of finding a bird's nest containing eggs, is a sign that you will have property left. If there are young ones in it, you will have a lawsuit about it and may lose it.

BIRTH.—For a married woman to dream of giving birth to a child portends that she will recover quickly from her confinement. For a single young woman to dream the same denotes that she is in danger of losing her chastity.

BLIND.—For persons in love to dream that they are blind, denotes that they have made a bad choice in the object of their affections; and that their association will by some unexpected cause come to an end. To dream of the blind is a sign that you will have few real friends.

BLOOD.—To dream of blood is very bad, if you see it upon yourself; if on others, it denotes loss of property, and severe disappointment. If expecting to be married, something will occur to prevent your union, and if you dream that your hands are bloody, you will be in danger of injuring some person. Beware!

BOAT.—If you dream that you are sailing in a boat or ship and the water is smooth and the weather pleasant, it is a lucky omen, denoting a prosperous business, and happiness in marriage. If the water is rough and muddy you will have to labour all your life. If you fall into the water you must beware of disaster.

BONES.—Dreaming of bones denotes poverty; if they are partly clothed with flesh, that you will grow rich by degrees, and ultimately possess a good deal of property. To dream of human bones foretells that you will become rich through the death of some relative or friend.

BOOKS.—To dream of books is a good sign; it denotes that your future life will be very aggreable. If a woman in the family way dreams that she sees a number of books, it betokens the birth of a son who will rise to eminent learning and great honour. For a young woman to dream of books indicates that she will be married to a very learned man.

BOOTS.—If you dream that you are wearing a new pair of boots and they hurt your feet, it is a sign that you will meet with great and painful difficulties caused by your own imprudence.

BOTTLE.—To dream of a bottle full of wine indicates your future prosperity; if the bottle is empty, it denotes that you have an enemy in possession of a secret, which if revealed will do you a deal of harm. To dream that you are drinking out of a bottle denotes that you are intending to harm some young person, which if perpetrated, will greatly injure your character.

BOUQUET.—To dream that a person gives you a bouquet of flowers, shows friendship. If you dream a young man gives you one it is a sign that you will marry him. If you dream you give one to a young woman it denotes you will marry her.

BOX.—If you dream that you are opening a box, and looking for something in it, and cannot find it, it is an indication that you are going to be troubled about money matters; or that you will suffer some pecuniary loss.

BOX.—To dream of the plant "Box," implies long life and prosperity, with a happy marriage and large family.

BRACELET.—To dream that you are wearing a bracelet, you will shortly be married to a wealthy person. If you dream that you find a bracelet it is a sign of a coming fortune; if you dream that someone put upon your hand a bracelet you will soon fall in love, and be accepted, or if already in love, you will be married without delay.

BRAMBLES.—To dream of briars and brambles and that you are injured by them, is a very unlucky dream; it denotes difficulties and problems to be overcome all your life. If you are not hurt by them, you will have trouble, but of a short duration.

BRANCH.—If you dream that you see a tree full of branches, it denotes abundance, and a numerous family—a happy posterity.

BREAD.—To dream of seeing a quantity of bread is a sign of sufficiency of worldly possessions. If you dream of eating good bread, you will enjoy good health, and live long; but if the bread is burned it is a bad sign. To dream of baking bread is also bad, generally denoting affliction and sorrow.

BREAST.—To dream that your head is reclining on the breast of another is a sign of true, valuable, lasting friendship and affection.

BREATH.—To dream you are out of breath, or have difficulty breathing is a sign that your health will be affected.

BREWING.—If you dream that you are brewing, you may expect the visit of some distant friend. It denotes also great efforts to secure your wishes, and that you shall succeed, and for a short time have both trouble and uneasiness, but all will end happily.

BRIDE, BRIDESMAID, OR BRIDEGROOM.—This is a dream of contradiction. To dream that you take any of these characters is very unlucky, it is a sure forerunner of grief and disappointment.

BRIDGE.—To dream thay you are crossing a bridge in the daytime, foretells a change of situation. If any person interrupts you, it implies that the one you love will deceive you; but if you pass along without any impediment, you will succeed in your undertakings, and prosper. If you dream that you are walking towards a bridge that is broken down, do not make any hasty change in your situation for the present, as you will not be successful.

BUGLE.—To dream that you are playing this instrument, is a token of joy, occasioned by great friendship and kindness from your relatives. To dream of hearing a bugle sound denotes unexpected news from abroad of a very pleasing nature; and to married persons it denotes the birth of a child.

BUGS.—To dream of these creatures is a sure indication of sickness, and of many enemies seeking to injure you. To a young man it implies that his enemies are trying to deprive him of his job. To a young woman, that she has several rivals who do not hesitate to blacken her character. To a business man or tradesman, it denotes that he has persons in his employment who are robbing him.

BULL.—To dream that you are pursued by a mad bull, denotes that you have violent enemies, and that many injurious reports will be spread detrimental to your character; and that you will be in danger of losing your friends. If in love, the one you love will be in some great danger, and will narrowly escape some misfortune.

BURNS.—A dream of contradiction, implying health, happiness and warm friendship.

BUTTER.—To dream of butter, in any way, or form, is a good dream and indicates joy and feasting. To those in love it is a sign of early marriage. In litigation it betokens success; also in any controversy, or dispute. Your absent friend, if you have one, will come home safely, and be to you a friend in need. If you are exposed to any trial or danger, it betokens speedy deliverance.

CABBAGE—To dream of cutting cabbages denotes that your wife, or husband, as the case may be, is very jealous of you. If you dream of someone else cutting them, it is a sign that you have an enemy trying to create jealousy in the mind of the person you love. If you dream of eating cabbage, it denotes the illness of the object of your affections, and that you will suffer the loss of a sum of money.

CAB.—To dream of riding in a cab denotes a short illness, and speedy recovery by change of climate. It also denotes increasing prosperity.

CAGE.—To dream that you see birds in a cage is a sign that you will have an early and an agreeable marriage. If you dream you see a cage, the door open, and no bird there, it is a sign that the one you love will forsake you. To dream of seeing a person letting a bird escape from its cage, is a sign of an elopement.

CAKES.—If you dream of oat-cakes, it denotes health and strength; if of sweet cakes, of coming joy; if of making spicy cakes and bread, an approaching marriage, at which you will meet the one you will eventually marry. To dream of cakes twice, denotes your own marriage in which you will be happy both day and night.

CALM.—To dream of a calm succeeding a storm indicates the reconciliation of separated friends; the end of trouble; the comencement of peace.

CAMELS.—To dream of these wonderfully hard and patient creatures, denotes that you will have heavy burdens to bear, and disasters to meet, all of which, however, you will bear with heroism; but the time will come when you will be entirely rid of them, and become very happy.

CANARY BIRD.—If you dream that you hear a Canary sing, it denotes your marriage, and a comfortable home. It denotes that your partner will be cheerful and tender and very kind to you. If a married woman dreams she sees two canaries in a cage, it prognosticates twins.

CANDLES.—To dream that you are making candles, denotes that you will be very useful to others; if you dream that you are buying candles, it indicates feasting and rejoicing. To dream that you see a candle burning brightly, portends that you will receive a letter containing pleasing intelligence; but if you dream that you see a candle snuffed or blown out, it denotes the death of a friend.

CANNON.—To dream of hearing the firing of cannon, denotes personal troubles. To a young woman it denotes her future husband will have been a soldier.

CAPTIVE.—To dream of becoming a captive is a sign of insolvency. It is also a sign of an unhappy marriage, suffering from the bad disposition and misconduct of the wife or husband, as the case may be.

CAP.—To dream of a female with a fine cap is a sign that she is in love with you. But she would make a foolish wife. To dream you see a man with a cap on, denotes that the one you love is a silly fellow, and will care but little for you after the honeymoon.

CART.—To dream of riding in a cart denotes that you will come down in the world, and have many hard knocks. To dream of driving a cart indicates poverty.

CARVING.—To dream that you are carving meat for others denotes that you will be a benefactor; and to be carving meat for yourself denotes prosperity in your business; if single, that you will succeed in love.

CARPET.—To dream that you are in a carpeted room denotes advancement in your work and also to money.

CATS.—An unfavourable dream, denoting treachery and deceit. If a young woman dreams of cats it is a sign that her sweetheart is sly and very deceitful; if a young man dreams of cats, she whom he loves will be a vixen, and will be sure to wear the trousers. If a business man dreams of cats, it denotes bad and dishonest employees. To dream of a cat and kittens is a sign of a numerous family, but not too good; trifling and vain. To dream that you kill a cat is an omen that you will discover your enemies, and defeat their schemes.

CATTLE.—If you dream of cattle grazing in a pasture, it is a good sign of prosperity and affluence. If you dream of driving cattle it portends that if you are diligent and industrious, you will make money. Black and large-horned cattle denote many violent enemies.

CATHEDRAL.—To dream that you are in a cathedral denotes that you will have enough money to enable you to travel and see the sights of the world. To married persons, it denotes good children, some of whom will be eminent in the church.

CHAINS.—To dream you see chains is a token that enemies are trying to harm you, but that you will escape their meshes. If you dream that you are confined in chains, it betokens very severe trials for a time, from which you will eventually be extricated. To dream that a person puts a gold chain upon your neck indicates great favour; and to those in love marriage and happiness.

CHEESE.—To dream of cheese denotes deception and infidelity in a lover. If the cheese is full of maggots, it denotes numerous little meddling persons who will annoy you. To dream of eating cheese betokens regret for having acted unwisely.

CHERRIES.—To dream of cherries in winter implies disappointment in business, and in marriage, and deceit in love.

CHILDREN.—If a married woman dreams of her confinement, it denotes that she will have a healthy child. If a single woman dreams of having a child, her virtue will be threatened.

CHICKENS.—To dream of a hen and chickens is the forerunner of ill-luck; your loved one will desert you, and marry another. To a farmer, it denotes a bad season.

CHILDREN.—This a lucky dream, and denote success in business and increase of wealth; to dream that you see your child die, is a dream of contradiction; the child will recover. This is a good dream for speculation.

CHURCH.—To dream that you go to church in mourning, denotes a wedding; if you go in white, it denotes a funeral.

CLOCK.—To dream you hear the clock strike denotes a speedy marriage, and that you will be very comfortable in life. To dream that you are counting the hours, if in the forenoon, it indicates much happiness; but if in the afternoon, some misfortune and danger. If the clock strikes roughly, and not the full hours, it denotes an upset in your health.

CLOUDS.—To dream of dark clouds suspended over you, indicates that you will have to pass through great sorrows. But if the clouds break, and roll away, your sorrows will pass away, and prosperity will follow.

CLOTHES.—If you dream that you have plenty of clothes it is a dream of contradiction; you will want clothing. If you dream that you are naked, it is a sign that you will be well clothed. For a woman to dream that she is making children's clothes, it is a sign of maternity. If a sailor dreams that has lost his clothes by shipwreck, it is a sign of marriage.

CLOTHING.—See Apparel.

CLOVER.—I do not know a better dream than this. If you are in a field of clover, it is an omen that you will do well, be in good health, and very happy. If you are in love nothing can be more favourable, and all your undertakings will prosper and be advantageous to you. A very favourable dream for speculative ventures.

COFFEE.—This dream is favourable. It denotes a settled life, prosperity and great happiness in marriage. To a single person it promises a faithful, affectionate and loyal partner.

COFFIN.—It is a bad dream. It is a sign of the death of some dear friend. As to the community, it is a sign of great mortality.

COLOURS.—Dreaming of colours, flags, and banners streaming in the air denotes elevation from obscurity, and that you will be highly honoured.

COMBAT.—To dream of a combat with anyone, denotes rivalry, and that you will seek revenge. If you dream that your combat ends in victory, it is a sign that you will retain the affections of the one you love.

COMETS.—It is a bad dream. It is a sign of great calamity among the nations, as war, famine, and plague, and even cold-blooded murder. All persons, after such a dream, may look for misfortune. If you dream of a comet, do not travel, nor expose yourself where there is danger, nor undertake any hazardous enterprise.

COMMUNION.—To dream that you are partaking of bread and wine in church or chapel, is at all times favourable, it foretells many enjoyments. To the young girl it denotes virtuous love in him with whom she associates.

COMPANION.—To dream of your companion denotes abiding friendship.

CONCERT.—To dream of a concert is a dream of contradiction, denoting wrangling and disputes—disagreement among relations.

COOKING.—Dreaming of cooking denotes a convivial party, and also a wedding of some friend. It also denotes a family made happy by the abundance of this world's goods.

CORKS.—To dream that you are corking bottles, indicates that soon you will have cause to give a party on account of a favourable change in your fortunes. If you draw corks, it is a sign of the visit of some particular friend.

CORNFIELD.—To dream of cornfields, or corn, is a most favourable omen. It betokens health, a happy family, a prosperous trade, great wealth. Speculations will prosper. Love-life will be a perennial honeymoon.

CORPSE.—To dream you see a corpse predicts a hasty, inconsiderate, and imprudent marriage, in which the parties will be very unhappy. The children will be unhealthy, and have bad dispositions.

COW.—To dream that you are pursued by a cow, denotes an enemy; if you escape it, you will defeat your enemy. To dream of milking a cow is a sign of abundance. If a woman dreams of a cow calving, its a sign of a difficult confinement.

CRABS.—To dream of a crab denotes reverses, and to a sailor danger of shipwreck.

CROWN.—To dream of a monarch's crown, denotes favour with the great, and elevation in your state. To dream that you wear a royal crown is a dream of contradiction; it denotes your degradation. To dream that you give a crown, shows that you will rise to independence.

CROWS.—This is a sign of a funeral.

CRUCIFIX.—To dream of holding a crucifix indicates trials and crosses. If you hold it long, it denotes heroism in any future misfortunes.

CUCKOO.—This dream denotes temporary disappointments in love, even a rupture; but eventually you will secure by marriage the person whom you love. If you dream that you hear the cuckoo, and she stutters, it denotes that you will not succeed in business or love.

CUCUMBERS.—This is a dream of contradiction. As cucumbers are deemed unwholesome, it denotes health; for the afflicted to dream of cucumbers, it denotes speedy restoration to health. To a single person, it denotes a happy engagement, and eventually an agreeable marriage.

DAIRY.—To dream that you are in a dairy, making butter, denotes that you will be very fortunate in your secular concerns; that you will marry a plain, homely person, and be happy and have many children.

DARK.—If you dream that you are in darkness and cannot find your way, and you stumble, it denotes a change in your temporal affairs for the worse; by your imprudence, you will dreadfully commit yourself. But if you dream that you emerge from the darkness, and behold the sun, it denotes your ultimate escape; you will be happy, and regain your reputation.

DANCE.—This is a favourable dream; it indicates that you will be the recipient of great favour and honour; that your plans will succeed; that in love you will win the hand of the person you desire.

DEAD.—To dream of your relatives and friends who are dead, denotes personal or relative affliction, and also much mental suffering. If you dream that they are happy, it is a sign favourable to you.

DEATH.—This is a dream of contradiction; it augurs happy long life. To the single it denotes an honourable and happy marriage.

DEER.—This is an unfavourable dream. It portends quarrels and dissensions in which you will be a party. If in trade it denotes embarrassment and failure. It is a bad dream for the tradesman, and all official characters.

DESERT.—To dream that you are travelling across a desert, is a sign of a difficult journey, especially if you dream that the weather is wet and boisterous. If you see the sun shine, your journey, and all affairs, will be safe and prosperous.

DEVIL.—This is a shocking dream; and I fear that those who dream of him are too much akin to him. It is high time for them to mend their ways, for this dream portends great evil.

DEVOTION.—To dream that you are devotional, and at your devotions, is a good sign of bodily health, and temporal happiness.

DIAMOND.—This dream indicates solid and extensive wealth. Dreaming of a diamond also indicates happiness in love affairs.

DICE.—To dream that you are playing with dice, is a sign of great changes in your business and circumstances; it shows your life to be very chequered; and your enterprises very hazardous. If you are a female look well to the private character of your lover. Is he a gambler? If so, take care. To a young man, it denotes that he will lose the respect of those upon whom he is dependent.

DINNER.—If you dream that you are getting your dinner, it is a dream of contradiction. It foretells straits and difficulties, and that you will often want a meal. You will not be comfortable in married life.

DIRT.—To dream that your person or clothes are dirty, denotes sickness and sorrow. It also implies loss of virtue and reputation. To dream that someone throws dirt upon you, is a sign that enemies will try to injure your character. Beware of some in whom you are too confiding.

DISEASE.—To dream that you have a disease is a sign to a sick person of recovery; to the young man it is a warning against evil company, and intemperance. It is not a favourable dream for lovers. It denotes infidelity. If any have a lawsuit, this dream is a bad omen.

DISPUTE.—Disputes always foretell quarrels and dissensions, and impediments to your success in trade; yet all will be of short continuance, you will surmount every trial. To a lover, to dream of disputes shows some disagreement, which it will be difficult to make up.

DISTANCE.—To dream that you are at a distance from your friends, foretells family quarrels and alienation. To dream of any friend at a distance, indicates that you will hear of them shortly.

DITCH.—To dream of ditches is unfavourable. It betokens danger, losses, injuries, and your enemies trying to harm you. The lover who dreams that he or she falls into a ditch, is a sign that the contemplated marriage will be a bad one. For a tradesman to dream of falling into a ditch, it is a sign of money troubles.

DIVING-BELL.—To dream of a diving-bell is a happy omen; it indicates every kind of happiness—a brisk trade—a joyful family; and if in love, a successful consummation by marriage. You will be rich, virtuous, and well-liked.

DIVORCE.—This is a dream of contradiction. If a married person dreams of sueing for a divorce, it is a sign of the fidelity of his or her partner, and that there is no cause for jealousy.

DOCKS.—To dream that you are standing by the docks in a seaport town, denotes you will hear favourable news from abroad.

DOGS.—If you dream that a dog makes friends with you, you will meet with faithful friends. But if he bites you, your best friend from some cause, will become your greatest enemy. If it only barks at you, you will quarrel with your friend or lover.

DOVES.—This is a fortunate dream. It denotes progressive prosperity in business; permanent esteem and affection of friends, peace in the family. If you love, your love will be warmly returned. To the lover it denotes that his or her love is returned with all the fervour they could desire, that they will marry and be very happy for many years.

DRESS.—To dream of buying a dress, denotes advancement; and that you will obtain your wishes. To dream of being well dressed is a sign of the approval of your friends and lover.

DRINK.—To dream that you are drinking at a fountain, is a sign of much happiness and enjoyment. If the water is muddy, it denotes approaching trouble. If you are thirsty, and cannot find water, it portends that your trials will have to be borne without any assistance, you will need self-reliance. To dream that you give drink to the thirsty foretells your sympathetic heart and your benefactions when required.

DRIVING.—If you dream of driving a car, expect losses in trade. To dream that someone is driving you in a car is a good sign; it foretells a marriage. If you dream of driving any vehicle, it betokens your dependance, and poverty. To dream of driving an ass, is a sign that you will be tyrannical with your husband or wife, as the case may be.

DROWN.—To dream that you are drowning denotes overwhelming difficulties and losses in trade. If you dream you are drowning, and someone, or a lifeboat, &c., rescues you, it is a sign that some friend will efficiently help you in your difficulties and sorrows.

DRUM.—To dream you hear the sound of a drum, with its musical accompaniments is a sign of national and family turmoils, and disorders.

DRUNK.—To dream that you are drunk, denotes you will be reckless with your money, reputation, and domestic comfort. If a female dreams she sees a drunken man, it is a sign that her future husband will be intemperate.

DUMB.—To see a dumb person will bring many rewards from being mild and gentle.

DUST.—To dream that you are almost blinded with dust, indicates trouble in your business, and the dispersion of your family. But if in your dream you get clear of it, you will recover your former state.

DWARF.—This is a dream of contradiction. If you dream you see a dwarf, it is a sign that you will be elevated in rank. If you dream that you are a dwarf, it denotes health, muscular strength, and independent and commanding circumstances. To the tradesman, the farmer, and the lover, it is a lucky dream.

EARTHQUAKE.—This foretells much trouble to the dreamer: it indicates great losses in trade, and business; family ties death will dissolve; it also denotes family quarrels, the interruption of domestic happiness. I fear, too, it is a sign of national calamities, including commercial distress. It is a bad dream for lovers.

EARWIG.—An enemy! He will threaten to undermine the basis of your prosperity and happiness. He works very secretly. A rival! Mind he does not steal your lover.

EATING.—To dream that you are eating is an unfortunate omen portending family quarrels, separations of lovers, losses in trade, bad harvest, and shipwrecks at sea. To dream that you see other persons eating, and you with them, denotes choice friendship and eminent success in your trade or profession. If married you will be very happy, loving your wife, and be loved by her.

ECHO.—To dream you hear an echo to your own voice denotes that the letter you have sent will be met by a favourable answer, that the person to whom you have proposed will accept you; that your children will be beautiful, and good. Mind you do not idolize these little echoes! You will also hear of an absent friend.

ECLIPSE.—This is a strange dream. This omen is sometimes met in dreams, but is very rare. It indicates the illness of someone closely connected with you, and also the frustration of plans connected with the heart and marriage.

EDUCATION.—To dream of education in any way denotes your advance in literary fame. You will be much esteemed.

EGGS.—To dream of seeing a great number of eggs, indicates success in trade and in love. It also denotes a happy marriage and good children, and great prosperity. If you hope for advancement to a better job, or position, it shall be yours. To dream that the eggs prove rotten denotes unfaithful and treacherous friends and lovers. To dream of eating eggs portends great enjoyment.

ELDERBERRIES.—To dream of this fruit portends sickness. It denotes a very uncertain courtship.

ELEPHANT.—To dream of an elephant denotes health, and strength; and that you will associate with the good elements of society.

EMBROIDERY.—To dream of embroidery, denotes deceit in those who apparently love you.

EMPLOY.—To dream that you want employment is a sign of prosperity. To dream that you have abundance of employment, denotes that you will have nothing to do. To dream that you employ others, is a sign that, if you are not careful, you will injure them. This is a dream of contradiction.

ENTERTAINMENT.—To dream of a place of entertainment, is the fore-runner of some joyful festivity, where heart will meet heart. If you felt great pleasure in your dream, marriage will soon crown your wishes. If you felt unwilling to leave the entertainment, your marriage will be a very happy one. It is a good dream for business and speculation.

ENVY.—To dream that you are envied is a sign that you will be admired and loved; and that if you have a rival, he or she will yet be completely mastered. This is a dream of contradiction.

ERMINE.—To dream you see anyone arrayed in this beautiful and expens-ive fur, portends that you will rise to great honour and dignity. If you dream that you are arrayed in ermine, it denotes a great and magnificent state awaiting you.

ESCAPE.—To dream that you try to escape from any danger, and cannot, denotes continued trouble. To dream that you escape from sickness, from an enemy, from fire and water is a good sign; you will have trouble for a while, but eventually you will be triumphant. If you escape from a snake you should enquire into the character of your lover.

EVERGREENS.—Lasting happiness! Lasting Love! Lasting honour! Peren-nial domestic bliss! Fresh engagements will be crowned with success. Go to a new position, change your residence; you will be happy whatever you do.

EXILE.—If you dream that you are banished, it implies that you will travel a great deal.

FABLES.—If you dream that you are reading, telling, or hearing fables, it denotes that you will have agreeable friends, with whom you will have very agreeable association. To those in love it indicates that the partner is dissatisfied.

FACES.—If you dream that you see your own face in a glass, it is a sign that your secret plans will be discovered. If you see in dreaming many strange faces, it portends a change of your present abode, and associations. If you gaze in your dream upon the faces of friends, &c., it is a sign of a party, or wedding, to which you will be invited.

FACTORY.—To dream that you are inspecting a factory, when all is in operation, denotes that your trade will flourish, by which you will acquire much wealth, and be very useful all your life. It also betokens a time of commercial prosperity generally.

FAILURE.—This is a dream of contradiction. To dream that you fail in business—that you fail in securing the person you love—that your plans do not succeed, indicates that, by wise and cautious procedure, in all things you will succeed.

FAIR.—It is very unlucky to dream of being at a fair, it portends negligence in your business, and also false friends. The persons about you are not so honest as they should be. Through rivalry the lover is likely to suffer loss.

FAIRY.—To dream that you see a fairy, is a very favourable dream. Poor men have had this dream, and afterwards become very rich. Engagement and happy marriage will follow this dream by either sex. Indicates rapid rise for a man in his business or profession.

FALCON.—This is a very bad dream. There is a foe near you, full of envy, injuring you with the tongue, and mind he or she does not injure you with the hands.

FALL.—To dream that you fall from an eminence, from a tree, or the edge of a precipice, denotes a loss of situation, and of property. If you are in love, you bestow your attachments in vain; you will never marry the person. To the tradesman, it denotes a failing business, embarrassment, &c.

FALSE.—An unusual dream. It indicates the very reverse, true, firm, and lasting friendships; a lover not of mushroom growth, but like an ever-green, always perennial!

FAMINE.—This is a dream of contradiction, denoting national prosperity, and individual comfort, in wealth and much enjoyment. You will have many friends, a true lover, and a happy family.

FARM.—To dream that you are taking a farm, denotes advancement. Probably someone will bequeath property to you, and make you independent. If you dream of visiting a farm, and of partaking of its produce, it is a sign of good health. If you are single and unengaged, and a young person there serves you with something to eat and drink, you will soon be very agreeably in love.

FAT.—To dream of getting fat is an indication of illness and also of lovers' quarrels.

FATHER.—To dream of your father, denotes that he loves you; if he be dead, it is a sign of affliction.

FAWN.—For a young man or young woman to dream of a young deer, is a sign of inconstancy. If a married woman has such a dream, it portends fruitfulness.

FEVER.—To dream you have a fever denotes constant change in your business circumstances. They will alternate: sometimes you will be prosperous, sometimes poor. To dream that lovers both have a fever prognosticates that the attachment will be dissolved.

FIDDLE.—This dream is a sign of prosperity, and of great enjoyment. You will receive joyful news of a beloved distant friend. It is a sign that your love will be accepted, and will result in happy marriage, and good children. To dream that you are tuning and playing the fiddle, denotes your speedy marriage.

FIGS.—This is a favourable dream, denoting that you are likely to receive a munificent gift which will raise you to comparative independence.

FIGHTING.—This dream certainly portends disagreements and quarrels in families. It also denotes misunderstandings among lovers, if not temporary separation. If you dream that a person fights you and beats you, it is a sign that the malice of your enemies will be successful; if you beat him, that you will defeat the malignant policy of your foes.

FIRE.—If you dream of fire you have had a lucky dream. It betokens health and great happiness, kind relations, and warm friends. And if a young lady and gentleman should thus dream, then all that they wish for will be theirs. But if you dream that you are burned with the fire, it portends an accident.

FISHING.—To dream that you are fishing and obtain no fish is an omen of bad success in business, or in love. If you catch them, it augurs the acquisition of riches. If you see the fishes at the bottom of the water, it is a sign of wealth and grandeur.

FISH.—To dream of seeing a number of fishes of a choice kind, and delicious to eat, indicates that you will have much pleasure in all your engagements; you will be comparatively independent. If you dream that a fish eludes your grasp, slipping from your fingers, it betokens loss of job, of friends, and especially of a lover.

FLEAS.—To dream that you are annoyed by them indicates harm from evil and malicious enemies; business will decrease; friends prove false, and lovers unreliable.

FLOODS.—For seafaring persons, merchants, &c., to dream of floods is a favourable dream, denoting successful trade, and a safe voyage, but to ordinary persons, it denotes bad health, law-suits terminating unfavourably; also enemies, proving injurious. If you are a lover, your rival will, like a flood, sweep away from your embrace the object of your affections.

FLOWERS.—To dream that you are gathering beautiful and fragrant flowers, it is an indication of prosperity; you will be very fortunate in all you undertake. If in your dream, you bind the flowers into a bouquet, it portends your very agreeable marriage. If the bouquet gets loose, and the flowers appear to be scattered, your brightest prospects, and most sanguine hopes will be blasted.

FLYING.—To dream of flying denotes that you will escape many difficulties and dangers. It denotes success in trade and in love. Very likely you will have to travel. If you dream that you are trying to fly very high, it is an indication that you will aspire after a position which you will never reach, and for a job for which you are not qualified.

FOG.—It denotes great uncertainty. You wish to be accepted as a lover. It is doubtful. You have applied to your friends for assistance. They will never give it. You are speculating in shares, they may ruin you. The dream is unfavourable. If you dream that the fog clears away and the sun shines, your state will be happily reversed—uncertainty will vanish.

FORTUNE.—It is a dream of contradiction. If you dream that one has left you a fortune, it is a sign that he will not. If you dream that your friend has got a fortune, it is a sign of his coming poverty. It is not a good dream.

FOUNTAIN.—To dream you see a muddy fountain indicates trouble. To see a crystal-clear, overflowing fountain, denotes abundance, freedom from want. You will be highly respected and honoured. The person whom you love will love you, and your love will be permanent.

FOWL.—To dream of fowl denotes moderate comfort in temporal things; but in love, it denotes you will meet with slander and rivalry. Be on your guard.

FOX.—If you dream of a fox, you have a sly, lurking enemy—a competitor in trade determined to undermine your interests; and in love a rival determined to displace you.

FRAUD.—To dream that you have committed a fraud is a dream of contradiction, denoting the public appreciation of your character of integrity and honour. If a lover, you will discover the hidden acts of your rival, and gain the victory.

FRIENDS.—Dreaming alarmingly of a distant friend is a sign that sickness, or some upset, has befallen that friend. If your dream of distant friends be calm and pleasing, expect good news soon. Your lover will soon return, and it will end in matrimony. Dreaming you see distant friends rejoicing, denotes prosperity to them and to yourself. If they weep the dream is bad.

FRIGHTENED.—To dream that you are terrified at some object, or through any other cause, is a dream of contradiction. Terror implies bliss; fright, joy; pain, pleasure. Your bargains, contracts, &c., will be successful. If you dream that you overcome your fears, there will be a glorious turn in your affairs, and you will swim on the tide of prosperity. And, for doubtful lovers, all your fears will be turned into pleasures. It shows that your engagement will end satisfactorily, only persevere and do not be daunted by present appearances, however unfavourable they may seem.

FROGS.—Frogs are harmless creatures. To dream of them is favourable; it denotes success in business; to the farmer propitious season, and good crops, and healthy profitable cattle. To all classes, to young and old, it is a good dream, denoting good friends, and public patronage and support. To the lover it is a happy portent.

FROST.—This dream denotes very severe trials and troubles. If a female dreams it she is in danger of conquest through a deceitful sensual man, who will eventually desert her. To the man of commerce, it indicates difficulties in business.

FRUIT.—To dream of fruit has a different interpretation according to the fruit that you dream of. But to dream of a collection of numerous and varied fruits, both English and foreign, portends unbounded acquisition of wealth—and an agreeable and wealthy matrimonial alliance—a numerous and happy family. The different fruits have different prognostications.

GALA.—To dream that you are at a fête or gala, indicates that you will be so circumstanced in life as to be able to enjoy yourself by travelling to distant places. If you dream your lover is with you, it portends great married happiness.

GALLOWS.—This is a strange dream of contradiction. It denotes luck in all ways; good business—much money and a high position. For those in love, the achievement of all they desire.

GAME.—To dream that you are playing at a game, and win, is a sign that you will be unsuccessful. But if in your dream you appear to lose, it denotes you will be prosperous. If you are in love, you will obtain that person as your partner for life.

GAME.—If you see game in the woods, and shoot it, it is a sign that you will obtain the heart you covet. If you dream of abundance of dead game, it denotes a marriage. If the game is decomposing, it denotes the decay of health, and business. You will be disappointed in love.

GARDEN.—This is a very fortunate dream. One of the best. It denotes an abundance of everything. Good crops for the farmer, good trade for the business man. For those in love the achievement of all they desire. However, the dream must be of a well-kept garden full of shrubs and flowers.

GATHER.—To dream of gathering up money is a sign that your state will greatly improve. To gather fruit in season denotes great enjoyment, health, and happiness; but if out of season, it is grief without reason. It betokens enemies, and deceitful love. To dream you gather flowers, denotes that you will marry early and happily.

GHOST.—To dream you see a ghost, and the sight appals you, is a bad omen. Difficulties will come upon you, and they must be fought. Enemies will try to injure you. But if you are bold in your dream, and see the ghost vanish, it denotes that you will overcome all.

GIANT.—A difficult dream to encounter. It means that you must meet an enemy; but meet him boldly face to face and your giant will disappear.

GLOVES.—To dream that you lose your gloves denotes loss in business, and loss in trade, a change of abode awaits you; if you dream that you lose your right-hand glove, if married, you will lose your partner; if single, another will deprive you of your lover.

GOATS.—You will have enemies, and many trials through deceit; but your mind will be happy under all; your trials will not sink you, but operate for your good. And you had better be happy in adversity than miserable in luxury and splendour.

GOLD.—This is a dream of contradiction. It signifies poverty and distress. Beware of speculation. It is a bad sign to dream that the person you are going to marry has plenty of gold.

GOOSE.—This is a bad dream, for a single man. The woman whom he loves will prove a very silly incompetent wife; she will be a gossip, never at peace with her neighbours, and always quarrelling with her husband and his relations. He had better surrender her to someone else.

GOOSEBERRIES.—See *Fruit*.

GRAIN.—To dream that you see a quantity of grain is a most fortunate omen, it implies that by industry and perseverance you will become wealthy and be greatly respected and honoured. To the farmer it denotes favourable seasons, and good crops. If you are in love it will lead to a successful marriage, and you will have a numerous and happy family.

GRAPES.—See *Fruit*.

GRASS.—To dream that you see green grass, is an omen that denotes great and continued prosperity; if you dream of withered and decayed grass, the dream is a sign of sickness and distress.

GRAVE.—To dream of an opened grave is a sign of the dissolution of some near friend or relative.

GUN.—To dream that you hear the report of a gun, forbodes that you will hear of the death of a distant friend or relative; it also portends that you may be slandered by your enemies. But like the report of a gun, that opposition will soon pass away. If the lover dreams of hearing a gun, it denotes a rival determined to supplant you. It also denotes bad luck to a business man, he will have losses through fraudulent debtors.

HAIL.—To dream that it is hailing or snowing, is a bad dream. It denotes disappointed hopes, and blighted prospects. To the farmer unpropitious seasons, and poor crops. To the lover unsuccessful application. To persons in business heavy losses. Even friends will disappoint your expectations.

HAIR.—If you dream that you have luxuriant hair, it denotes continued health and prosperity. If you dream that your hair is falling off, to a man it is the portent of bad trade. If you dream that your hair turns grey, it is a sign of bad health, of a poor business, and the decline of a lover's affection.

HAMMER.—To dream that you hear the sound of a hammer denotes a brisk trade, and great gain. To the operative it is a sign of full employment, and good wages, and of good health, to enjoy the same. To a young woman it prognosticates an agreeable husband who will be industrious, temperate, and most likely to rise in the world.

HANDCUFFS.—A bad dream, denoting that if you are not watchful over your propensities, you will fall into temptation and crime, for which you will suffer severely. There is a bad prospect before you. Therefore take care to avoid this position. If a lover dreams of being handcuffed to another person, it denotes miserable matrimony.

HANGING.—To dream that you are being hung, denotes good to you. You will rise in society, and be wealthy. To dream that you see a person hanged, is an omen of good to him. He also will attain wealth, and great honour.

HARES.—To dream that you see a hare pursued by dogs, is not a good sign; it portends enemies; but you will be able to escape. To dream you see a few hares, denotes choice and faithful friends. If a hare runs towards you, it denotes the visit of a dear friend. To those in love it is the portent of an early and happy marriage.

HARMONY.—To dream that you hear musical sounds floating in the air, or that you listen to harmony of any kind, is the portent of a long and happy life. In love it denotes that your lover is most amiable and affectionate, and sincerely attached to you. Marriage to you will be a happy boon. This dream is a good omen for everyone.

HARVEST.—To dream of harvest time, and that you see the reapers in the cornfield reaping the corn and binding it in sheaves, is a most favourable dream. You could not have had a better. It denotes prosperity to the farmer especially, many customers for the tradesman, and lucrative bargains to the business man. If a lover dreams of harvest it prognosticates the consummation of his or her wishes, ending in an early marriage.

HAT.—To dream you have a new hat portends success in any scheme. To dream that you lose your hat, or that another takes it off your head, you have an enemy not far off who will both openly and secretly seek to do you injury. To dream someone puts your hat on his head, foreshows a rival; or it denotes that someone is possessing some property which certainly belongs to you.

HEAVEN.—To dream of heaven denotes a change of worlds, and that if you regard your dream, the remnant of your life will be spiritually happy. Do not forget this significant dream.

HEDGES.—To dream of green hedges is a sign of agreeable circumstances. If the hedges are flowery, it betokens great prosperity, and success in love. If you cannot pass on your way for thorny hedges, it denotes that in business, you will suffer through competition, and in love, by determined and ruthless rivals.

HELL.—This dream forbodes bodily suffering and mental agony, arising from restless enemies, loss in business, &c.

HERMIT.—If you dream that you have become a hermit and retired from the world, it indicates that you will have failures in business, be reduced in your circumstances, and experience some mental depression, but that eventually you will rouse yourself, and surmount every conflict and difficulty, and become wealthy; but to the young it denotes that their marriage is an uncertainty.

HILLS.—To dream of ascending a high steep hill and you are unable to arrive at the top, it is a sign that you will have to labour and toil all your life, and have many difficulties and troubles to overcome. It denotes that those in love will not find their path easy.

HOME.—To dream of the home of your childhood, and the scenes of your action in it, in company with your former play-fellows, indicates your continued health and prosperity. To those in love it betokens a true and responsive love, a happy marriage, and great marital happiness. You will have numerous children, and each child will do well.

HOMICIDE.—To dream of committing this dreadful crime, is an evil dream, it portends many severe misfortunes and heavy losses. It is an adverse dream in all walks and outlooks of life; business, love, &c.

HONEY.—To dream you are eating honey denotes good health, long life, prosperity and great enjoyment. Your business will be all you can wish, lucrative, raising you to independence. It denotes that your lover is virtuous, sincere, and very fond of you. It would be death to part from you. It denotes that the husband, or the wife, will be of a sweet disposition, industrious, affectionate and faithful.

HORN.—To dream you hear the sound of a horn denotes intelligence from an absent friend in a distant country, though not of an agreeable nature. If you hear the sound repeatedly, it is a sign of disagreements.

HORSE.—Dreaming of this noble animal is generally good. To dream that you are riding a handsome and good horse betokens future independence and happiness. But if it throws you, it denotes that your purposes will be thwarted. If you dream that horsemen approach you, it foretells that you will receive news from a distant friend. To dream of white horses, denotes a marriage, yours, if you are riding upon it.

HOUNDS.—To dream of following the hounds indicates that your pursuits will not be very productive, and that the person you are in love with will disappoint you.

HOUSE.—To dream you build a house, foretells prosperity and success in business. After such a dream, you may expect a great increase, with better profits.

HUMMING BIRDS.—This dream denotes travel to a foreign country, and great success in business, or profession there. If you dream of a large flock of humming-birds, it foretells that you will be very fortunate and save money; if you see one dead, you will not succeed, but return to your own country.

HUNTING.—To dream that you hunt a stag, and capture it, is a good sign of secular prosperity—to the lover, a sign that he will obtain his wish. To dream of hunting a hare denotes misfortune and trouble, and especially disappointment in love. To dream that you are hunting a fox, denotes wily competitors or rivals; if you kill him, it portends your triumph after severe contention.

HUNGER.—To dream that you are very hungry denotes that by your genius and industry you will rise in the world to wealth and honour; to the lover, that your sweetheart will undertake a journey before you marry; in business, prosperity.

HURRICANE.—This dream always foreshadows evil. Danger to the traveller, and disappointment to the dearest lovers. It augurs ill for the business man, and it is the precursor of family feuds and quarrels.

HURT.—To dream of having hurt yourself, or that someone has hurt you, is a dream of contradiction. It implies that your projects will succeed whether as a lover or a person in business; and that all the malicious attempts of your enemies will prove abortive.

HUSBAND.—To dream you have one, is a dream of contradiction; your wish will not be granted. To dream you fall in love with another woman's husband, indicates loose desires, and disregard to virtue. But for a widow to dream that she has a husband, and that he smiles upon her, indicates that she will soon have an offer, and it will be accepted.

ICE.—Dreaming of ice is always bad. It foretells failure in trade, unsuccessful speculation and enterprise. It indicates that your now ardent lover is about to cool down and jilt you. To the sailor it denotes disasters at sea. It is a bad dream for the farmer auguring devastation of crops.

ICICLES.—If you dream you see icicles suspended betokens good luck. If a man he will shortly marry a girl of great beauty and accomplishments, who will be very much attached to him. They will have a large family of girls, who will have their mother's beauty and marry rich men. To a young woman it predicts a marriage with a man of wealth, and they will have a large family of boys, who will rise to eminence.

IDIOT.—This is a dream of contradiction. It indicates that you transact business, and have friendships that you will receive advantages from, or marry, an intelligent person. To dream that you are an idiot, foretells your competency for every future engagement.

ILL.—To dream that you are labouring under any illness, denotes that you are in danger of falling into a great temptation, which, if you do not resist, will injure your character. If you are not careful your rival will supplant you.

IMPS.—This dream betokens grief and vexation. The persons around you will very much annoy you. It indicates false and malicious and revengeful persons. Those in love are treading on dangerous ground, and too much trust may lead to a broken heart.

IMPRISONMENT.—This is a dream of contradiction. It prognosticates liberty in every sense, and enjoyment in respects, especially in marriage.

INFANCY.—If a married woman dreams of infancy, it indicates a state of pregnancy or a desire for same. To dream of your own infancy, denotes good fortune in trade or profession, or in courtship and matrimonial affairs. To dream you are an infant again is bad.

INDIGENCE.—To dream that you are in indigent circumstances is a good omen, it denotes the receipt of a large sum of money, and is generally the forerunner of a fortunate occurrence. If a pregnant woman dreams of being in poverty it foretells she will have a son who will become a great man, and acquire wealth.

INFIRMARY.—To dream that you are in an infirmary, denotes an accident or sickness. To dream you leave it, is a sign of recovery. To dream that you are visiting the patients therefore shows an elevation in your position, and a feeling and generous heart.

INJURY.—To dream that some person or persons have injured you, denotes enemies who have evil designs against you.

INK.—To dream that you are using ink denotes prosperity in business; if you spill it, and dirty your hands, it denotes that your correspondence will not be successful, whether in trade, or in love. You must expect an unfavourable answer.

INN.—It is unlucky to dream of being at an Inn, it denotes poverty and want of success in your undertakings. To the tradesman it denotes loss of money, and a falling off in business. If you are in love, it portends that your sweetheart will jilt you and marry another.

INSANE.—This is a dream of contradiction. It is a good dream, followed by good health, domestic happiness, rare social enjoyment, and long life. As to the lover, it shows extraordinary affection.

INSTRUCTION.—To dream that you are receiving instruction, prognosticates that you will shortly be placed in circumstances as to need the advice and assistance of your friends, and it will be well if they come to your assistance. To the lover, it indicates a dangerous rival, under which rivalry you will need help and consolation. To dream that you give instruction, denotes that your friends will be placed in a similar state, and will require your advice and aid.

INSULT.—To dream that a person insults you, denotes that you will lose your lover through a silly and trifling quarrel. It also portends that what occurs will go in opposition to your wishes and interests, and that you will be very unfortunate for some time after your dream, unless you rouse yourself, and change your place of residence.

ISLAND.—To dream that you are on a desolate island implies the loss of your lover. If it appears a fertile island, covered with vegetation, it implies that your present lover will prove unfaithful; but you will soon meet with a more favourable match.

ITCH.—To dream of having the itch is an unlucky dream, denoting much difficulty and trouble in business and love. You will marry a person of irritable and restless disposition, and are likely to be in adverse circumstances, and unhappy.

IVORY.—This is a good dream. To those in love it portends beauty, sweetness and rare enjoyment. Success for the business man and abundance for the farmer.

IVY.—To dream of ivy is a sign that your friend, your lover, your husband, or wife, will adhere to you as ivy clings to the wall. You will have good health and live long. Your enemies can do you no harm. In commerce and business you will prosper. For those in love an excellent dream, you will enjoy a happy household.

JACKAL.—This dream indicates that you have an inveterate, deep, and sly enemy who will leave no stone unturned to harm you, but much to his annoyance it will turn out for your advantage. While he falls you will rise; while he is disappointed, you will triumph. To dream that a jackal bites you, it implies you will be much annoyed by a rival who will steal the one you love. But your loss will turn out a happy one; though you may grieve at first.

JAIL.—To dream that you are in jail is a dream of contradiction. Prosperity in business, freedom from embarrassment, and domestic happiness will be your lot. If a young man dreams that he is in jail, it is a sign that he will succeed in life, and marry the girl of his choice, the loss of whom he has had reason to fear. To dream of escaping from jail, denotes to the person in distress, a favourable change in his personal circumstances. It also indicates the recovery of health.

JEALOUSY.—To dream that you are jealous of your husband or wife, or sweetheart, as the case may be, is indicative of trouble and great anxiety. If you are in business, you may expect your affairs to be very much agitated and interrupted from unforeseen causes, you will also experience many disappointments in money affairs, and trouble and annoyance on account of the failure of some with whom you do business. To dream that another is jealous of you, expect misunderstandings, distrust and altered affection. But do not despair, it will be all the better for you.

JEWELS.—It is always a good dream, the harbinger of great prosperity, and a great amount of wealth. To dream that the one you love gives you jewels is a sign that his affection is real, and that he will certainly marry you. If a young man dreams that he sees his loved one adorned with jewels, it foretells his speedy and happy union; that his bride will possess a sweet and lovely disposition. To dream that both you and your lover are counting and inspecting jewels, denotes numerous healthy, and fortunate offspring.

JOURNEY.—If you dream that you have to journey to some distant country, it foretells a great change in your circumstances. If the journey is pleasant such will be the change in your circumstances. If rough, and unpleasant, it is an unfavourable sign.

JOY.—This dream is a sign of good health, and that you will receive a sum of money, or become rich through the inheritance of an unexpected legacy from a distant relative.

JUDGE.—To dream that you stand before a Judge, indicates that you will be involved in some dispute, or have some serious charges made against you. It is a dream of contradiction; for if you dream that the Judge acquits you, it indicates your discomfiture; if he condemns you, it augurs that your plea will be successful, and you will triumph over your enemies.

JUMPING.—To dream that you jump, augurs that you will meet with many impediments and trials; but by industry, courage, and perseverance, you will eventually surmount them. If a single person, it also implies that you will have a sweetheart much attached to you, but whose parents will oppose your union.

KERNEL.—To dream of a good kernel, portends favourable circumstances. To dream of an unsound rotten kernel denotes that you will discover a false friend.

KEY.—To dream that you lose a key, denotes disappointment and displeasure. To dream you give a key denotes a marriage; to find or receive one, the birth of a child; to dream of many keys, denotes riches, as the result of a flourishing business.

KILL.—To dream you see a person killing any fowl, bird, or animal portends that your loved one will place his affections on another, and will desert you. To a married woman it announces that some false friend of her husband will make improper advances to her.

KING.—To dream of being in the presence of monarchy, and that you speak to a sovereign, indicates that you will rise to honour and dignity in your country. If the monarch is unfriendly, the dream is unfavourable, and your expectations will not be fulfilled. If a young girl dreams that she is in company with a king, it foretells that her future husband will be well off, and probably occupy a situation under government.

KISS.—To dream of kissing one whom you should not, is a bad sign; it denotes a false friend, or a false lover. To see another kiss your fiancee, portends a rival. To see your loved one kiss another person, denotes false love from a false heart. To dream that your lover kisses you with affection, and repeatedly, shows him to be true to you, and that his intentions are good. For married persons to dream of kissing each other, portends that you will meet with an unfaithful companion.

KITE.—To dream you see a kite flying high, portends elevation in your station in life. If you are flying it yourself successfully, and if it flies high and steadily, it is a good sign. You are sure to rise above your present position; some high official station will be yours. In love it is a good dream, especially for a widow. It frequently foretells travel in distant countries. The farmer may expect large crops. But if the string should break, and the kite be blown away, all your enchanting prospects will be blasted.

KITTEN.—To dream that you are playing with a kitten, and that it scratches or bites you, denotes that your sweetheart has a trifling mind, and is of a spiteful disposition, and that if you marry you will have an unhappy life, and wish yourself single again.

KNAVE (*at cards*).—To dream of playing at cards, and that you continually hold the knave of diamonds in your hand portends seduction. The knave of hearts, you will meet with a lover; the knave of spades widowhood, and the knave of clubs debt and trouble.

KNIFE.—This is an unfavourable dream. If you see knives cleaned ready for a feast, it is a contradictory sign, a portent of poverty. If you see them bright and sharp, it denotes your enemies, and their evil designs against you. If you are married, your partner will prove false to you; and if you are in love your sweetheart will reject you and marry another.

LACE.—If a young man dreams that his sweetheart is adorned with lace, it shows to him that she will be very extravagant and improvident.

LADDER.—This dream has great import. You will reach the top of the ladder of the ambition to which you aspire. If in business you will prosper. It is the portent of wealth, honour and glory. Scholars and students will reach the climax of their ambition. Farmers will have good crops. All in all an excellent dream.

LAME.—To dream that you are lame implies that your future life will be one of difficulties and disappointments, and that your means of subsistence will be limited and sometimes precarious. Your life will indeed be a warfare.

LAMENT.—To dream that you are lamenting any loss in trade, or by death, is a dream of contradiction, you will have cause to rejoice on account of the acquisition of some property, or the good conduct of your children. To dream that you hear others lamenting denotes good luck to your friends or relatives and that you will rejoice with them. I see also that it is the precursor of a wedding.

LAMPS.—If you dream that you are carrying a bright lamp, it foretells that in your particular calling you will succeed, and be highly thought of. To those in love it is a good omen. If you dream that you carry a lamp with a dim flickering light, it denotes illness. To dream of seeing many bright lamps denotes a coming festivity. If you appear to be exultant on the occasion, it denotes your marriage.

LAND.—To dream that you possess land is a good dream. It is indicative of wealth and independence. To dream that you give notice to quit land, foretells change of residence, probably in a far country. If you dream that you receive a notice to quit, it betokens reduced circumstances.

LARK.—It is very lucky to dream that you hear the singing of a lark. It denotes good health and prosperity. If not married it shows that your future partner will be rich, and that you will live in the country, and will have many children who will be a credit to you while you live. In all probability, some of your children will be talented musicians and vocalists.

LAUGHING.—To dream that you are laughing immoderately denotes vexation and disappointment. If you are in love it is a certain sign that it will not be reciprocated. The affection of your sweetheart is not decided; it oscillates between you and another. Therefore be cautious how you act. Curb the passion of love; you are likely to be jilted. Laughing is often a sign of weeping and sorrow.

LEAD.—To dream of lead denotes troubles and quarrels. If in love there will be contention between you. If married it denotes that the affections of your partner are on the decline. It also foretells family quarrels, and separation, and great discomfort. An unpleasant dream.

LEAVES.—Dreaming you see the trees covered with beautiful fresh leaves, is good. Your affairs will prosper. You will succeed in business. It is a rare good dream for those in love, indicating full and continued affection. If you dream you see blossoms, and then fruit among the leaves, it denotes your marriage, and a large family. If the leaves appeared withered, ready to fall off, it is not a good omen; it portends losses in trade, bad crops to the farmer, and disappointments in love.

LEARNING.—To dream of being in a place of learning shows that you will attain influence and respect by your future diligence and hard work. It is a good omen to dream that you are learning, and easily acquiring knowledge.

LEAPING.—If you dream of leaping over any impediment, it denotes that you will easily surmount every obstacle to advancement, and eventually reach the top. Persevere, and the victory is sure. To persons in love, it shows many impediments and dangers, and also rivals; but if you dream that you leap over any obstacle, it foretells that you will win those whom you love, and be happy.

LEASE.—To dream of taking a house, shop, warehouse, or any other building on lease, foretells great success in trade, and that you will soon live together in marriage with the one you love.

LEG.—To dream you have bruised, dislocated, or broken your leg, or lost the use of it, foretells that a young woman will marry a man of intemperate and indolent habits, and who, through his improvident and unsteady conduct, will always be hard-up. It shows to a young man that he will marry a tender-hearted female, but rather irritable, and not a good manager in household affairs.

LEGACY.—This is a lucky dream, always prognosticating the reception of some good fortune. The lovers' union will be a happy one; secular pursuits will be successful; farming occupations will prosper.

LEMONS.—To dream you see lemons growing on a tree denotes that you will visit a foreign land, and probably marry a native of it. To dream that you eat lemons denotes you will be attacked by a dangerous illness, from which you will recover. To dream you see a great number of lemons, denotes that your marriage, though pleasant for a while, will not live up to your expectations.

LENDING.—This is not a good dream. You will be surrounded by a good many needy dependants, who will annoy you and keep you short of money. It is the omen of losses.

LEOPARD.—To dream of these beautiful, yet savage creatures, indicates travel to a foreign land, where you will have to encounter many dangers and difficulties. But you will eventually overcome them, marry well, and be very prosperous and happy. It is likely that you will stay there all your life.

LETTER.—Dreaming of receiving a letter sometimes indicates presents, or at least the reception of unexpected news, from a person you have not heard of for many years. To dream that you send a letter, denotes that you will soon be able to perform a generous action.

LIGHT.—To dream you see a light, of a brilliant nature, denotes riches and honour; if you see it suddenly extinguished, it denotes a setback in your affairs.

LIGHTNING.—It is a favourable dream, for it augurs success in business and advancement to honours and independence. To the farmer it portends good seasons, and abundant, and well-harvested crops. To those in love it denotes constancy in affection, and a speedy and happy marriage. If the lightning be attended with storm, rain, hail, and thunder, the dream will not be so favourable.

LILY.—To dream you see this lovely flower, is a sign that by your virtuous and industrious career, you will be very happy and prosperous. To those in love it denotes the virtue of the object beloved. The lily is the emblem of purity; therefore it augurs well. If you marry, you will be happy, and have lovely children. If in your dream, you see the lily wither, then your expectations will be nullified.

LINEN.—To dream that you are dressed in clean white linen, denotes that you will shortly receive some good tidings; that the one you love is faithful and sincere, and will soon bring matters to a point. It is an omen of great success in business, and of large crops to the farmer, and of domestic felicity. If your linen appears in your dream to be chequered, you are likely to have a legacy left you. If it appears to be dirty, it is the omen of disappointment in love, rivalry, jealousy, &c.

LION.—This dream denotes greatness, future elevation. You will occupy some important and honourable position. To a young woman it foretells that she will be married to a man of superior intellect, and amiable disposition. To a young man, it denotes that his future wife will be no waster, but intellectual, of great spirit, and efficient in household affairs. She will be a help-meet for him indeed.

LIQUORS.—To dream that you drink brandy, is a certain sign that you will emigrate to, and reside in, a foreign land, in improved circumstances. If you dream that you drink rum, it portends that you are to be a "sailor's bride," or the bride of one who obtains his livelihood by shipping. If you dream that you drink gin, it foretells that you will live in a large and populous town, and have to struggle. Dreaming of drinking whisky prognosticates a sudden reversion in your circumstances, and loss of valuable friendships. You will need more than human support.

LOCKS.—To dream of locks implies that difficulties will hinder your success. If you see cabinets, drawers, &c., with locks and no keys, it is a bad dream for the business man, and for those in love. You cannot effect your object. Your hope is sweet but it will never ripen into fruition. Should you dream that you find keys which open the locks, and you open them, changes the omen of your dream. You will succeed—you will acquire—you will rise. Young woman, or young man, the heart of the one you love is yours. It cannot swerve. Cherish it lovingly.

LOOKING-GLASS.—To dream that you look at yourself in a mirror, indicates that your business is not conducted on sound principles, and must ultimately fail, if you do not properly arrange it. It indicates also that you are surrounded with deceitful persons, whom you will soon discover. In trying to injure you, they unmask themselves. Do not be too confiding, nor be led away by flattery. Try to discover motives.

LOCOMOTIVE.—To dream of a railway-engine, foretells travel, or the arrival of an old friend.

LOVE.—To dream that you see *Cupid*, the god of love, and that he smites you with his arrow, is a sign that someone loves you, and will soon appear; and the same dream denotes the same to a young man. To dream you do not succeed in love is a dream of contradiction; you will succeed, and marry, and be happy. To dream that your friends love you, foretells future prosperity in business, and great domestic happiness. To dream of being in company with your lover is a good dream. You will soon marry the object of your choice, have many children, who will be to you a source of comfort and joy. To a woman with child it foretells a safe delivery of a lovely child. To dream of loving and being loved, denotes that you will enjoy a large circle of loyal friends ready to assist you in any emergency, and be faithful at all times. It foretells to the farmer propitious seasons, heavy crops and much wealth.

LUCKY.—To dream that you are lucky is a dream of contradiction. It is the omen of disappointment, and misfortune. After such a dream, be cautious, and keep your eyes open. Let judgment, and not your passions, rule.

LUGGAGE.—If you dream that you are travelling, and that you are encumbered and annoyed with a great deal of heavy luggage, it foretells great trials and difficulties which will cause you much trouble and expense. This will almost overwhelm you, and you will be in financial trouble, principally caused by the insolvency of others, or the bad treatment of your relatives.

LUMBER.—To dream that you are surrounded and annoyed with lumber, foretells trouble. To dream that you are searching among lumber, and find something valuable, foretells the acquisition of a fortune, which will completely reverse your circumstances.

LUTE.—To dream that you hear the sweet tones of a lute, foretells the receipt of good news from a long-absent friend, or from one whom you ardently love. It also denotes to the lover that the person beloved is true, of amiable and engaging manners, and great sweetness of disposition. To a young woman it shows that her lover is devotedly attached to her, and is good tempered, sincere, and constant, but not very rich. They will marry, and have lovely children who will do well. Such a dream foretells a happy old age and good health; and in all cases it is the fore-runner of success and happiness.

LUXURY.—To dream of living in great luxury is a sign of poverty, and that you will meet with many disappointments. You are not likely to be successful in trade, and will have many obstacles to overcome. In love it denotes rivalry, jealousy, and quarrels, between lovers.

MACKEREL.—To dream that you see these fishes in the water very clearly, foretells success in business, prosperity and good fortune. If you dream of bad mackerel you will never marry your present sweetheart, for she will prove worthless, being false-hearted.

MADNESS.—To dream you are mad or in company with mad persons, portends well for the dreamer; even vigour of intellect, great efficiency in commercial transactions and adequate remuneration, even to the acquisition of wealth. The business man, the tradesman, and farmer, after such a dream may expect an uncommon tide of prosperity. It also betokens good health and long life. It is a good omen for all affairs concerning the heart.

MAGIC.—Dreaming of magic foretells changes and revolutions. Some change will take place in your circumstances, but it will be a change for the better. It indicates also that your hitherto trusted friend will be caught in acts of treachery and injustice, but you will triumph over that enemy. Your present love, and that of your sweetheart, will abide only a little longer. Both of you wish for a change. Make the change, it will be better for you.

MAGISTRATE.—To dream that you stand charged with crime before a magistrate, is bad, if he convicts you; if he pronounces you free, the dream is a sign of good. If you dream that you are created a magistrate it foretells future advancement to a high official station, with great honour, and large emoluments.

MAGNET.—To dream that you see a number of magnets foretells that your path will be laid with snares; mind you are not ensnared with such fascinations.

MAGPIE.—To dream that you see a magpie, foretells that you will soon be married. To dream that you see two magpies, it denotes that you will be married twice.

MAP.—To dream that you are inspecting a map indicates that you will have to leave your native land and reside many years in a foreign country, but eventually you will return to your own country. If you inspect a plain map you will return poor; but if it be a coloured map, you will come back wealthy, and enjoy a happy old age. If a female inspects a map in her dream, it indicates that her husband and her sons will be great travellers.

MARIGOLDS.—To dream of marigolds denotes a constant lover, and a happy marriage; also elevation in position, accumulation of riches and honours, and great success in your undertakings and constancy in love.

MARINER.—To dream that you are a mariner, intimates that very likely you will emigrate to some distant part. To dream you see a number of mariners, portends news from abroad; and to the man of business it indicates successful bargains and seafaring transactions. If a young woman dreams of mariners, and one in particular, it foretells that a sailor will be her husband; if she dreams of a mariner in distress at sea, it is a dream of contradiction; her husband will return safely.

MARKET.—To dream that you are in a market denotes a good job, competent circumstances, and high domestic enjoyment. It denotes some approaching happy event, which will be the cause of joy and feasting. If a female dreams that she is in a market, where many look at her, it is a sign she will have many in love with her, and it will be difficult for her to decide which to take.

MARRIAGE.—To dream you see a marriage is very unfavourable to the dreamer; it denotes trouble and misfortune, and the alienation of a lover. To dream that you assist at a wedding, portends some pleasing news, indicating advancement in life for you.

MARSH.—To dream that you are walking in a marshy country, portends a troubled life. If you can scarcely get along for swamps, it denotes sorrows and difficulties. But if you get on easily and out of the marsh soon, it foretells that the remnant of your days will be passed in comfort. To those in love this dream shows many scrapes and trials, but ultimate triumph over every obstacle and foe.

MARTYR.—To dream of the age of the martyrs denotes that you will be firmly attached to the verities of the Christian religion, and be in intimate alliance with the good things of the earth. To dream that you are a martyr, is indicative of your unwavering defence of the truth, and your triumph over all hostility.

MASK.—Should a young person dream that his or her sweetheart appears to them wearing a mask, it is a sure sign of insincerity and deceit. It shows double dealing, a pretending of love to you, while engaged to marry another. Learn to discriminate and to ascertain motives.

MASTIFF.—To dream you see a mastiff, is a sure sign that someone whom you suspect of infidelity is, after all, your best friend. If you dream that you are bitten by a mastiff, it prognosticates that some pretended friends will cause you harm, especially in love affairs; they will anxiously strive to supplant you in the affections of your sweetheart. If a girl dreams of a mastiff, it shows that her lover is faithful and true.

MAYPOLE.—To dream that you dance round the Maypole, or that you are watching others dance round one, announces the advent of some joyous occasion.

MEADOW.—To dream that you are walking through a meadow, predicts good fortune to you. If a young girl dreams that she is walking with a young man in a meadow, it is a sign that her beau will be very loving, that he will marry her, and acquire riches, and by him she will have a fine family, and will be very happy and live long. To a young man, it denotes that he will marry a beautiful and rich young lady, who will be devotedly attached to him. They will have a large family characterised by honour and happiness.

MEASLES.—To dream that you have measles, denotes that riches are about to drop into your lap from a quarter which you did not expect to yield anything. It also implies returning health and business prosperity.

MEDICINE.—To dream that you are taking medicine, and it tastes nauseous to the palate, implies that something will occur to you that will be very annoying and unpleasant for a little time only, and then be of much service to you. The dark clouds will vanish, and light appear. It is a good dream.

MELONS.—A young man, or a young woman, who dreams of melons is destined to marry or be married to a rich foreigner, and to live in a foreign land. Such a union will be crowned with great happiness, be attended with great wealth; their children will be few, but they will be virtuous and happy.

METALS.—To dream of gold denotes great trials, loss of property, and money troubles. To dream of silver foretells that you will meet with deceitful persons, and disappointment in love. To dream of copper coins, denotes poverty, and to dream of the metal, denotes accidents during travelling. To dream of iron indicates that you will marry a person of great spirit, and that you will acquire great wealth through your own industry, and successful speculations. To dream of lead portends the loss of your lover.

MICE.—To dream of mice indicates many meddling enemies and slanderers, also unsuccessful undertakings. It also foretells an unfortunate marriage and disobedient children.

MICROSCOPE.—To dream that you are looking through a microscope, denotes that you will discover some lurking and deceitful enemy, who will appear to you in real character, no longer under a disguise; also that you will be separated from your lover by moving far away; but you will meet again in happy wedlock, and have many children.

MILK.—To dream that you drink milk, foretells joy. To dream of selling milk, denotes bad trade, and disappointments in love. To dream that you give milk, denotes prosperity, and a happy marriage. To dream that you see it flowing from a woman's breast, denotes marriage, and a very large family. To dream of milking a cow, foretells abundance to the farmer, healthy cattle, and good crops.

MINCE-PIES.—To dream of eating mince-pies intimates that you will have to be at a wedding. To dream that you are making mince-pies, portends that you will soon be making preparations for your marriage. Your partner will be tolerably well off, though not affluent.

MISFORTUNE.—To dream that some misfortune has happened to you or your lover, is a dream of contradiction, foretelling that a person will be very fortunate in business, and have a very happy selection as far as a love mate is concerned. You will rise in life, and be greatly respected and esteemed. In married life you will be very comfortable; your children will be numerous, healthy, and a source of comfort to you.

MONEY.—To dream that you pay money, foretells your competency to do it through a prosperous business. To dream that you receive money foretells the birth of a child; it generally portends prosperity. To dream you find money foretells sudden advancement through a prosperous business and by marriage.

MOON.—To dream of the moon, foretells unexpected joy, and success in love. If it be a new moon it is a good dream for the tradesman, and farmer, and for affairs of the heart. The full moon denotes marriage; it is good for a widow.

MOTHS.—To dream of moths indicates enemies, who are doing you great injury, and labouring to undermine your position in life. It also portends that your lover will hear reports about you that will cause a quarrel between you, and probably a separation. To persons in business it indicates that you have dishonest and unfaithful employees who are injuring you in your business.

MOTHER.—To dream that you see your mother and converse pleasantly with her, denotes your comfort and prosperity through life. If a female, who has a sweetheart, dreams that she has become a mother, it is a sad dream.

MOUNTAIN.—To dream that you are ascending a steep and rugged mountain, shows a life of toil and effort; all your endeavours to better yourself will be made difficult by unforeseen events.

MOURNING.—This is a dream of contradiction. It portends good concerning you. Your lover is genuine, entirely devoted to you, and is sure to marry you, and to make you very happy. To the married it denotes much comfort, and to the business man it denotes great prosperity. The farmer will reap abundantly.

MURDER.—To dream that you have committed murder, is an awfully portentous dream. It foretells a vicious life, the perpetration of evil, and probably imprisonment. After such a dream, take care that you are not led along these paths by unscrupulous persons.

MUSHROOMS.—To dream that you are eating mushrooms denotes personal illness. To dream that you are gathering them, foretells the accumulation of wealth.

MUSIC.—To dream you hear delicious music is a very favourable omen; it denotes good news from a long-absent friend; to married people it denotes sweet-tempered children; in love, it shows that your sweetheart is very fond of you. Rough and discordant music denotes trouble and annoyance.

MYRTLE.—To dream you see a beautiful and fragrant myrtle, denotes agreeable circumstances. To a young person it foretells a very suitable and agreeable lover, a very pleasant courtship, leading to the altar. It portends a legacy to the dreamer. If a married person dreams of a myrtle-tree, it foretells that he or she will be married twice, and the second time to a person who has been married before. Also, you will have a very numerous family, most of whom will grow wealthy.

NAKED.—To dream that you are naked is a bad omen, foretelling trouble and misfortune. If you are a farmer, you will have bad crops, and you will lose many of your cattle, and suffer by robbery. To those in love it foretells that they will never marry those whom they now court; but another person of disagreeable temper, arbitrary, selfish, and tyrannical. To married persons it foretells infidelity in a partner.

NAME.—To dream that you have changed your name, is a sign that you will never be married.

NECKLACE.—To dream that you are wearing a rich and costly necklace, portends that you will speedily make a conquest of a very wealthy person; the courtship will pleasantly continue, till consummated by happy marriage. If a female dreams that she breaks the necklace and loses the beads, she will become poor in her old age.

NECTAR—To dream that you are drinking nectar foretells that you will accumulate riches and honour, and that you will rise beyond your most sanguine expectations. It also shows that you will marry well and live well to an old age.

NETTLES.—To dream of nettles prognosticates good health, and worldly prosperity; but to dream that you are stung by nettles indicates disappointment. You will be deeply hurt by the ungrateful conduct of some pretended friend; and if you are in love, your sweetheart will be liable to deceive you and to marry your rival.

NEWSPAPER.—Dreaming that you are reading a newspaper shows that you will hear good news, from a distant friend, which will cause you to quit your present employment, but you will benefit from the change. You will be able to commence business on your own account, in which you will have great success. If you are a single man, it portends that you will marry a widow. To persons in love it shows that the object of their affections will travel to a distant part of the world, and it will be many years before they are again united, but their reunion will be a very happy one. To the politician, it betokens great and stirring events in the nation. To the farmer it shows a favourable season.

NIGHTINGALE.—To dream of hearing this sweet-singing bird, is a very propitious omen, and may always be regarded as the harbinger of joy, success, and prosperity.

NIGHTMARE.—To dream that you have a nightmare signifies that you are under the influence of a foolish and imprudent person.

NOISES.—To dream of hearing great and alarming noises foretells domestic quarrels and dissensions. You will be alienated from your best friends and have trouble with your relatives. If you are in love, it portends that through bad influence, the one you love will abandon you.

NOSE BLEEDING.—To dream that you are bleeding at the nose, denotes that you will have an illness. To persons in trade it denotes bad trade and some losses. If you are in love you may expect that the one you love will prove unfaithful to you and marry your most intimate friend.

NUN.—For a young female to dream that she has entered a nunnery, and become a nun, prognosticates disappointment in love. It also warns her to beware of seduction, and not to put undue confidence in the faith of man. Try hard to investigate the motives which actuate him.

NUTS.—To dream of nuts having good kernels, is a good omen, denoting that you will become wealthy through the possession of a good legacy, and that you will marry an agreeable and rather affluent person. That you will live to a good old age, and be highly respected by a large circle of friends and acquaintances.

OAK.—To dream of a large oak with beautiful foliage is a very good dream. To the man of business it indicates a steady and permanent trade, and that you will be able to endure and surmount all difficulties. To a family it denotes constant and abiding domestic happiness. It also forebodes a happy, hale, and robust old age. To a young man it portends that he will commence business and succeed, and that he will marry a pretty and intelligent woman, of resolute disposition, very efficient in domestic management, and very industrious. To a young woman, it foreshows that her future husband will be handsome, having a strong and robust constitution; he will be very industrious, and enjoyment of his family, and especially their education and moral training, will be his major consideration. To dream of an oak full of acorns, foretells of unbounded prosperity. To dream of a withered and decayed oak indicates that your brightest prospects will not come up to expectations.

OCEAN.—To dream that you gaze upon the ocean when it is calm, is good; when it is stormy and turbid, it augurs ill. To dream of sailing on the ocean when it is smooth, and the weather calm, with favourable breezes, certainly denotes the accomplishment of a purpose, and any object devoutly wished for, obtained. After such a dream happiness and satisfaction will follow. It prognosticates success in love affairs. To lovers, it foreshows that they will have a delicious courtship, and sail straight on into the harbour of matrimony. Your wishes will meet in one another, and you will have mutual and endearing affection.

OFFICE.—To dream you are turned out of your office, foreshows loss of property; to those in love it indicates want of affection in their sweethearts.

OLD MAN.—For a woman to dream she is courted by an old man, is a sure prognostic that she will receive a sum of money, and be successful in her undertaking. For a young girl to dream of it, shows that she will marry a wealthy young man and have several children.

OLD WOMAN.—For a man to dream he is courting an old woman, and that she returns his love, is a very fortunate omen, it prefigures success in wordly concerns; that he will marry a beautiful young woman, have lovely children, and be very happy.

OLIVES.—To dream that you are gathering olives, denotes peace, delight, and happiness in domestic life, and in every situation. To dream that you are eating olives, foretells that you will rise above your present circumstances, whatever they may be; that you will obtain the favour and patronage of influential men, who will be the cause of your finding a profitable situation and acquiring wealth. For a person in love to dream of olives, either gathering or eating them, foretells that the person who addresses you is characterized by sincerity and truth. You will have a happy married life, attended with great prosperity.

ONIONS.—To dream that you are eating onions portends the discovery of a valuable treasure, or lost goods and money. To dream of paring onions and to have your eyes affected thereby, denotes quarrels with your friends, or with your family, which will upset you. To dream that you are getting onions, denotes that a friend will recover from illness.

ORANGES.—This dream is generally unfavourable. It foretells personal and relative illness and misfortune; also misunderstandings and family jars. To those in love, dreaming of oranges foretells coldness on the part of your lover, and growing indifference, and ultimate abandonment. If you are married, and dream about oranges, it denotes an unhappy marriage. In commerce, it foretells losses through the dishonesty of those employed. And to the farmer they indicate a bad harvest.

ORCHARD.—To dream that you are in an orchard, gathering fruit, agreeable to the taste, as well as pleasant to the eye, foretells that you will be made the heir to some property, and become rich. If the fruit appears ripe, your advancement will be immediate; if green, it is yet in the distance; but it will come.

ORGAN.—To dream that you see an organ, and hear it playing in a place of worship, predicts to persons in business great prosperity; and to the farmer a bountiful harvest. To persons in love it portends fortunate marriage, with a very suitable partner, and children who will grow up to be very popular.

OVERBOARD.—To dream that you have fallen overboard at sea, denotes illness and poor success in your undertakings. If also forewarns you that some friend, or perhaps the one you love, will turn against you, and by duplicity and misrepresentation will cause you much unhappiness. You will be in danger of sinking under the blow; but you will eventually surmount it, and be happy with another. To a farmer it prognosticates disease amongst his cattle, and his poultry.

OWL.—To dream that you see this bird of night, and that you hear it howl, denotes illness and disgrace. After dreaming of an owl, never expect to meet with continued prosperity, to marry the one you love at the moment, or to succeed in your present undertakings.

OX.—To dream that you see a herd of oxen is the harbinger of great prosperity and success in your engagements, particularly if you see them grazing, in which case it denotes the accumulation of immense wealth, and your elevation to honour and dignity. To those in love, it presages a happy and fortunate marriage, and that your partner will have a legacy left by a wealthy relative. To dream that you are pursued by an ox foretells that you will have an enemy or rival, who will annoy you.

OYSTERS.—To dream of eating oysters foretells that after many conflicts, and heavy losses, you will acquire wealth and independence; that married persons will enjoy domestic happiness, and that those in love, by patiently waiting, will obtain their wish by a happy marriage.

PAIN.—This is a dream of contradiction. If you dream that you suffer great pain it denotes the advent of some particular event, by which you will benefit greatly. To persons in business it foretells that there will be a great advance in their activities and that they will make handsome profits. To those in love it is an omen for good, foretelling the arrival of the propitious time when they will marry partners possessing an ample fortune. To the farmer it foretells a very congenial and rich season.

PALACE.—To dream that you live in a palace is a good omen, foreshowing that you will emerge from your present obscurity, and rise to a state of wealth and importance. To those in love it portends an agreeable partner, and a very happy marriage.

PANCAKES.—To dream that you are eating pancakes denotes the fruition of hope, and the arrival of some joyous occasion, that you have long been expecting. In matters of love it foretells that you will be married shortly, and that your partner will be loving, industrious, and eager to make you very happy. If you are trying to turn a pancake, and cannot succeed, it shows failure in love.

PANTOMIME.—To dream that you witness a pantomime at a theatre, implies that you live among deceitful persons; and that those who profess to be your friends, and flatter you, and speak well to your face, are deceitful at heart, and are working to injure you as much as they can. You will soon find them out, as in reference to business and love matters, they will shortly develop their real characters.

PAPER OR PARCHMENT.—To dream of paper or parchment implies that you will get into some kind of trouble. To dream that you can see clean paper, denotes that the affection of your friend or lover is unquestionably sincere. To dream of dirty, scribbled, or blotted paper shows the reverse; also unjust and dirty actions. If the paper is properly written on, it portends good bargains. If folded up, or chrushed, it denotes disappointments; if neatly folded, that you will obtain your wish.

PARCEL.—To dream that you receive a parcel denotes good fortune. You will either hear from a friend, or receive a present; if you dream that you are carrying a parcel through the streets, it denotes great changes in business, and a possible loss. It also denotes disappointment in love matters, and that the one you love will marry another person. If those in love dream of receiving a parcel, it is a favourable omen, denoting success in love.

PARK.—To dream of walking through a park, indicates health and happiness, and true friendship. To a person in commerce it is the harbinger of a flourishing business. If you dream that you have the company of another person with you, it denotes a speedy marriage. The now apparent obstacles will all vanish. Such a dream is very good for a scholar, or a person employed in scholastic affairs.

PARLIAMENT.—To dream that you are a member of the House of Parliament, foretells advancement. To dream that you are only a visitor, and that you listen to the debates, foretells family quarrels and dissensions, also that you will quarrel with your sweetheart and friends.

PARROTS.—To dream you hear a parrot talk, foretells that you will have a very talkative person for your companion. To dream that you see many parrots foretells that you will emigrate to a foreign country, where you will settle and marry, and be very happy. You will cultivate land and by it amass wealth, and secure some honour. You will only have two children, a boy and a girl; the latter will be married to a rich man; and the former will hold an official position and be held in high esteem.

PARTRIDGE.—To dream that you see a flock or covey of partridges foretells troubles and misfortunes; but·if they fly away, it portends that you will overcome them all and be happy. Partridges also denote enemies and false friends who will endeavour to create prejudices against you, and to sow dissensions between you and the one you love.

PATH.—Walking in a straight path denotes success in trade, in farming, and in love matters; if married, it denotes that a female will have a safe delivery, and that the whole family will be happy. If, in your dream, the path appears crooked, and filled occasionally with thorns, it foretells disappointments and treacherous friends.

PEACOCK.—To dream that you see a peacock with its feathers spread, denotes an unsound and uncertain position in life, and that you are surrounded with seeming friends, but who are deceitful. If you see the bird with its feathers not spread, it foretells a young man that he will marry a beautiful wife, and attain wealth and honours; and that a female will marry a handsome man, and live in ease and comfort, but she will have no children.

PEARS.—To dream of pears prognosticates great wealth, and that you will rise considerably above your present position. For a female to dream of pears, denotes that she will marry a person far above her rank. To persons in business, this dream denotes success, the accumulation of wealth and independence. It also foretells constancy in love and happiness in the marriage.

PEAS.—This is a good dream. To dream that you are eating them, denotes great prosperity. If you dream that you see them growing, it foretells good fortune in love, and a happy marriage. To dream of dried peas, foretells the acquisition of wealth.

PERFUME.—To dream that you are using a perfume or that you smell its rich fragrance, is always a favourable dream in reference to business and in love matters.

PHANTOM.—To dream that you see a phantom denotes that your expectation of the success of your plans will be disappointed. Appearances may flatter you; but in vain. You think that you have secured the affection of the one you love, but a rival will come and supplant you. It also denotes a quarrel with your best friend, which will cause you much sorrow. It also forebodes danger by travel, and loss of money by lending, and by giving too much credit.

PHEASANTS.—To dream that you see pheasants flying across your path, or in a field or plantation, foretells that a relative or friend will leave you a legacy. If you dream that you see them fight, and fly away, you will be in danger of losing your legacy by a lawsuit.

PICTURES.—To dream of pictures is not good, it indicates falsehood and deceit. It does not matter how beautiful the pictures may appear to you in your dream, it foretells troubles arising from false friends, who will malign your character, and try to damage your reputation. If you love anyone, as your future partner, that person is false, however gracious and loving he or she may be. That person has been attracted by another. Therefore, try to ascertain *motives*. To persons who are married it foretells the infidelity of their partner.

PIGEONS.—To dream of seeing pigeons flying in the air or otherwise, prognosticates that you will receive important news; they also denote a happy and suitable partner, and constancy and happiness in love. Also great success in trade, and the acquisition of wealth thereby.

PINEAPPLES.—To dream of pineapples portends an invitation to a feast or wedding, where you will meet a person you will afterwards marry. You will marry well and happily, and have a fine family who will all be successful when they grow up. It also foretells great success in business transactions. To the emigrant it bespeaks a safe voyage, and contentment and happiness in the country where he will settle.

PISTOL.—To dream that you hear the report of a pistol, foretells trouble. If you dream that you are firing a pistol, it foretells that you will marry a person of hasty and passionate disposition, but very industrious. It also foretells that your marriage will be moderately happy; that you will have many children who will do well in the world; particularly the first-born, who is sure to be conspicuous in the world, and be renowned for some great accomplishment or gift of nature.

PLAY.—To dream that you are at a play, where you have much amusement betokens happiness in the marriage-state, and extensive success in business. To a young man, or woman, it portends that they will marry well. To dream that you are taking part in a play, is not a good dream.

PLOUGHING.—For a young woman to dream that she sees a young man ploughing is a good omen, denoting that her future husband will be honest, sober, and industrious; and will by his own efforts and perseverance make a success of life. If a young man dreams that he is ploughing in a field, it foretells him that he will become very wealthy through his own exertions and industry. It also indicates much happiness in married life.

PLUMS.—To dream that you are gathering green plums, foretells illness in your family. To dream that you are gathering ripe plums in their season is a good dream for all. To dream that you pick them off the ground and they are rotten, denotes false friends, and a deceitful lover, and also a change in position. If you dream that someone gives you ripe plums, and you find them good to eat, it foretells that you will find a pleasant partner, that you will marry, and have a very comfortable home.

POISON.—To dream that you have taken poison foretells a reversion in your circumstances; it denotes that your business will be unremunerating, and that you will suffer through the dishonesty of others. If you dream that you recover from the effects of poison, it is a sign that you will extricate yourself from difficulties, and do well. If your dream that another offers you poison, it foretells treachery in the one you love; but, though you will be disappointed, you will soon find another far superior.

PRISON.—To dream that you are in prison is a dream of contradiction. It indicates freedom, happiness, and unbounded scope in business. In love, it foretells that you will marry a person whom you have known for a long time, but whom you have not regarded in the light of a lover. To dream that you are putting someone in prison, foretells that you will be invited to the wedding of an acquaintance or relative.

PROVISIONS.—To dream that you are hungry, and require provisions, and cannot obtain them, foretells want. But to dream that you have plenty of provisions stored up implies a future state of well being, and in probability, it foretells a long journey, either by sea or land, and that you will be in some dangers; but that you will overcome them all, and in foreign land acquire wealth, and return with it to your native land.

PUBLIC HOUSE. —To dream that you are keeping a public house denotes that you will be driven to extremities in your temporal affairs, and be compelled to act against your inclinations. To dream that you are drinking in a public house, is a bad omen, indicating illness, and probably debt. In love it foretells deceitful treatment by someone you love, who will very coolly abandon his attention towards you. In business it foreshows losses.

PURSE.—If you dream that you find a full purse, it foreshows great happiness, particularly in love; and that you will marry a person with property by whom you will have a numerous family. To dream of losing a purse foretells your own illness or that of someone you love.

QUAILS.—It is an unlucky dream, denoting bad intelligence, and family quarrels. It also shows that you will lose your lover through false and artful rumours. It also tells you to beware of false and deceitful friends and lovers. It is not an omen of happy matrimony.

QUARRELS.—This a dream of contradiction; for if you dream that you quarrel with some person, it foretells success in business or in love, and that you will enjoy much wealth, and a happy married life, notwithstanding all opposition.

QUEEN.—To dream that you are in the presence of the queen foretells advancement to a high position in life. This will be effected principally by your efforts; also you will have many friends. To a young woman it shows that she will marry a person holding a high official situation in the State, that they will have a numerous family, become rich and will be happy.

QUICKSAND.—To dream that you are walking amongst quicksands, implies that you are surrounded with many temptations, but you are not aware of them. It is to be feared that you will run into many dangers through your own imprudence and hasty conduct, and perhaps damage your reputation.

RABBITS.—To dream that you see rabbits implies that you will soon have to reside in a large and populous city, where you will marry and have a very numerous family. It also foretells that you will have a flourishing business, that your plans will be successful, and that you will triumph over your enemies. For a married woman to dream of rabbits, indicates increase of family.

RACE.—To dream that you run a race on foot, betokens the defeat of your competitor; it foretells your success in business. You will secure the affections of the one whom you so ardently love. You need not fear a rival, you will marry and be happy.

RAFFLE.—This dream of chance foretells bad associations and habits. You will sustain the loss of character, trouble in your business, and meet treacherous people, false love and disappointment in matrimony.

RAIN.—To dream of rain generally foretells trouble, especially if it be heavy and attended with boisterous winds. To dream of gentle spring rain, is a very good dream, denoting prosperous circumstances and happy love.

RAINBOW.—This is a token for good. It portends change, but a change for the better.

RAVENS.—This is a bad dream. It declares that trouble is coming, that mischief is brewing; you will suffer through injustice, and have to contend with much adversity. In love it shows that your lover is false, and your partner is to be suspected.

RICH.—To dream that you are rich is a dream of contradiction. You will be poor for a long time; but will gain money in the end.

RING.—If a married woman dreams that she loses her ring off her finger, it portends the infidelity of her husband, and that he is under the influence of another woman. If a female dreams that her wedding ring breaks, it foreshows trouble with her marriage; and if she dreams it presses her finger and hurts her, it forewarns her of the illness of her husband, or some of the family. To dream someone puts a ring on your finger, foretells union with the person you love.

RIVER.—To dream that you see a broad, rapid, and muddy river denotes troubles and difficulties in love and business; but if the river appears calm, with a glassy surface, it foretells great happiness in love, happy marriage, beautiful children, and commercial prosperity.

ROSES.—To dream of roses in their season is the omen of happiness, prosperity, and long life. If the roses are full and fragrant, it foretells to a young man who dreams it that his future wife will be fair and beautiful, intelligent and amiable, and that their union will be a happy one. It is a good dream for the business man and for all, prognosticating great success. If the roses are decayed, however, it indicates trouble.

SAILING.—To dream that you are sailing in a ship on smooth water, foretells, prosperity; on a tempestuous sea, misfortunes. To sail to, and arrive at, a pleasant country, denotes happiness in marriage. To dream that you are sailing in a small boat, and that you gain the harbour, foretells that you will make a rapid fortune.

SCHOOL.—To dream you are a master or mistress of a school indicates that you will not be well off. If single, that your intended marriage will be characterised by some opposition.

SERPENT.—This foretells a deadly enemy bent on doing you harm. If you are in love, there is a rival full of envy and malice, who will work to displace you. Indeed this serpent has already fascinated, and your star is beginning to wane; you are hurt by artful insinuations, and falsehoods, but do not let such treatment destroy your peace and happiness. To dream that you kill a serpent, portends that you will overcome your enemies and be successful in love, matrimony, and business.

SHAVING.—To dream that a person is shaving you, denotes a treacherous lover; and great disappointments; if you are married it denotes infidelity and discord; and to the man in business, it foretells losses.

SHEEP.—To dream you see sheep feeding is a portent of great prosperity and enjoyment. To dream you see them scattered, denotes that you will meet with persecution. To see sheep-shearing indicates riches, by marrying a person with money.

SHIPWRECK.—To dream you suffer shipwreck betokens misfortunes. To those in love great disappointment. To dream that you see others shipwrecked, is a dream of contradiction; you will see the elevation of some friends, or relatives.

SHOES.—To dream that you have got a new pair of shoes, is a sign that you will make many journeys. If you dream that your shoes hurt you, it denotes that you will be unsuccessful in your engagements. It is a bad sign for those in love. If you dream that your shoes take in water, it portends the falsehood of someone you love. To dream that you are without shoes, denotes that you will pass through life with comfort and honour. To those in love it betokens virtue, sincerity, and ardent affection for those concerned.

SHOOTING.—To dream that you are shooting a bird, and succeed, is very portentous. It denotes that the business man will accomplish his purpose; that those in love will secure the company and marriage with the person desired. But if you dream that you shoot and miss, it is a bad portent. It denotes that in business you will be unsuccessful. To dream that you shoot game foretells elevation to a state of wealth, and domestic happiness. To dream that you shoot a bird of prey is a sign that you will conquer your enemies.

SHOP.—To dream that you keep a shop is a sign of moderate comfort. You will have to succeed by industry and perseverance. To dream that you are serving with another person in a shop, indicates that you will meet with a marriage partner of agreeable personality; and that you will strive together very hard, and at length succeed in acquiring independence.

SILK.—To dream that you see silk, or buy, or sell silk, is an omen of good fortune to the business man. If the lover dreams of seeing a female in silk, it foreshows that his future wife will be wealthy and most ardently and sincerely attached to him. If a female dreams she is dressed in silk, it foretells that her future husband will be in good circumstances, and that both will move in good society.

SILVER.—To dream that you are collecting small silver coins, foreshows distress; if large coins, you will be engaged in some lucrative trade. To dream that you are paying silver for goods which you receive, or of receiving silver for goods which you sell, denotes a prosperous trade, though limited. To dream that your silver turns out not real, foretells a false friend, or lover.

SINGING.—It is a dream of contradiction, and foretells cause for weeping. It is portentous whether you dream you sing yourself, or hear others sing. If you love, it portends that the object of your affection will cause you grief by loving another in preference. To dream that you hear others singing denotes distress among your friends and relatives, and that you will suffer through their misfortunes.

SNAKES.—This dream denotes sly and inveterate enemies, who will conspire against you, and cause you much trouble. It foretells that you will have a false lover, who will leave you for another. To dream that you destroy a snake, denotes that you will overcome your enemies, and all your rivals in love.

SNOW.—To dream that you see the ground covered with snow is a sign of prosperity, and that you will maintain an unblemished character in spite of the attempts of your enemies to blacken it. To dream that you are walking upon snow with the girl you love, foretells that she will be very beautiful. To dream that you are in a snow-storm and very much harassed, is a good dream. You will have difficulties, but you will overcome them, and come out unscathed.

SOLDIERS.—To dream that you are a soldier, foretells that you will abandon your present employment, and change from one thing to another. It is a bad omen for a young woman; she will marry a worthless man, with whom she will experience much trouble. To dream you see soldiers fighting, denotes that you will be concerned in some serious arguments.

SUN.—To dream of seeing the sun foretells success in obtaining wealth, and success in love. To dream that you see it rise, denotes good news; to see it set, disagreeable news to the business man and losses. To dream that you see the sun overcast, is a sign of trouble, and great changes.

TEETH.—To dream that you see a person with white regular teeth, denotes that you will have a beautiful lover whom you will marry. To dream that your teeth are very loose, portends personal illness; to dream that one of them comes out, denotes the loss of a friend or relative. To dream that you have the toothache is a dream of contradiction; it denotes much social enjoyment and pleasure. To dream that you cut a new tooth, denotes change of residence, and to the married an increase of family.

TEMPEST.—This dream indicates troubles, and losses but you will surmount them and recover from them. It also indicates persecution, but your enemies can do you no harm. Those in love need not fear rivalry, for the object beloved is above all temptation, however enchanting.

TENPINS.—To dream of playing this game implies great fluctuations in business. You will have to struggle to avoid losing money. It also denotes hollow friendships and disappointments in love and marriage.

THIEVES.—To dream of thieves, is a bad dream; it denotes loss in all cases.

THORNS.—To dream of thorns, portends grief and difficulties.

THUNDER.—To see lightning, and to hear loud peals of thunder, implies that you will be exposed to danger, from which good friends will extricate you. You should be on your guard after such a dream.

TOADS.—This dream, to a business man, denotes ill-disposed competitors in the same line of business, and determined opposition from them. For those in love to dream of a toad, or toads, foretells that the object of your affection is mean, undecided, and inconstant, and not invulnerable to the advances of others. To dream that you kill a toad, denotes success and triumph in all cases.

TOMBS.—To dream that you are walking among tombs, foretells marriages; to dream that you are ordering your own tomb, denotes that you will shortly be married; but to see that tomb fall into ruins denotes the reverse, and also trouble to your family. To dream that you, with another person, are admiring tombs, denotes your future partner to be very suitable for you. To dream you are inspecting the tombs of the illustrious dead, denotes your speedy advancement to success.

UNFAITHFUL.—To dream that your friend, partner, or lover, is unfaithful, is a dream of contradiction; they will be just the reverse. But to dream that you are unfaithful, denotes the approach of some peculiar temptation which may put you to a severe test.

VAULTS.—To dream of being in vaults, deep cellars, or places underground, signifies that you will marry someone who has been married before.

VIOLIN.—To dream that you hear the music of a violin, foretells some social gathering, at which you will be a guest. It may be a marriage, the birth of a child, or the return of a friend from abroad. To see dancing with the music denotes prosperity, and marriage in the not too distant future.

• VIPER.—Can this be a good dream? Certainly not. It indicates that you have many enemies around you, who will strive to injure you. It denotes an unfaithful partner.

VISION.—To dream you see places, property, valuables, in a vision, denotes disappointment.

VOICE.—To dream that you hear merry voices, foretells distress and tears. To dream you hear the sound of woe prognosticates cause for joy. To dream that you hear many voices in conversation indicates some joyous event.

VOLCANO.—To dream of a volcano, foretells great disagreements, family rows, and lovers' quarrels. If you are planning to revenge yourself on anyone, the injury will rebound upon yourself. To a man of commerce, it portends dishonest employees, and a robbery, or some unfortunate event. It also implies civil disorders. To those in love it is a sign that all deceit and intrigue, on one side or the other, will be exploded.

VULTURE.—To dream you see a vulture, is a really bad dream. It is evident that some enemy or enemies are seeking to destroy your character and reputation. Let those in love beware. There are unscrupulous rivals everywhere.

WAR.—This is not a good dream. It foretells to the business man much competition and rivalry in trade. To a family it portends an occurrence which will interrupt domestic peace and happiness. It indicates great mutation in health and in circumstances; poverty frequently following wealth, and vice versa, and health often interrupted by sickness. If a female dreams about war, very likely she will be the wife of a soldier; and if a pregnant woman dream of wars, it is a sign that her next male child will rise up to become a soldier.

WEALTH.—To dream of wealth and affluence is not very favourable. It has frequently been found to denote the contrary.

WEDDING.—To dream of a wedding, portends a funeral near you. To dream that you are married, is a dream of contradiction; it denotes a life of bachelorhood. To dream that the one you love is married to another, foretells that you will be jilted.

The Origin & History Of The Original Old Moore

THE WORTHY DOCTOR was born and lived in the Parish of Southwark, London, where he practised Medicine and Medical Astrology. He was attached to the Court of King Charles the Second as a Physician and was indeed a popular figure in Court circles. His original *Almanack* was published as a black and white Broad Sheet, printed in old English type, and included instruction for the making of herbal remedies by country folk, based on his knowledge of Medicine and Astrology in relation to the months of the year and diseases in those days which attacked the populace from time to time.

The background of the *Almanack*, so called, is extremely interesting. From evidence to be found at the British Museum, it would appear that the first almanack saw the light of day some three thousand years ago, in the reign of Rameses the Great. It was produced by its originator in the form of a parchment document and was inscribed with many curious hieroglyphics. Much space was devoted to religious ceremonies, and reference was made to certain charms. Birthday information similar in character to the birthday delinations found in more modern almanacks was included.

There is no trace of any other almanack having been published until the year 173 A.D.; but it is hardly likely that this was so, and doubtless there is evidence in existence which would tend to prove that the almanack was carried on by other astrologers, both before and after the advent of the Christian era.

From the latter end of the second century to the beginning of the eighth, almanacks had become comparatively numerous, and the almanack makers of those days devoted much space to religious festivals and Saints days. It is said that the priests were responsible for the Biblical phraseology.

The Norman period saw the almanack produced in very highly-coloured and finished state, and some exquisite copies may still be seen in the libraries of the famous European cities. The effect of the many varied colours used is extremely beautiful. These rare and expensive almanacks contained lists of lucky and unlucky days and notes on such subjects as astrology, medicine, and occult research.

The first English almanack was published about the year 1495, and a copy is now to be found in the Bodleian Library, Oxford.

The year 1697 is an interesting date in the history of almanacks, for it was not until Dr. Francis Moore published his Broad Sheet in this year that the question of prophecies was seriously dealt with by the compiler. At that time, the great universities in England were also responsible for the production of almanacks. But shortly after his death in 1715, in London, the original *Almanack* as produced by Dr. Francis Moore was taken over and published by the City of London Liveried Stationers Company until the nineteenth century, when the House of Foulsham acquired the copyright and issued a popular edition of Dr. Francis Moore's *Almanack*, which is now known in its popular format as *Foulsham's Original Old Moore's Almanack*.

The Almanack *is always published some months in advance of the year for which it is dated, since the essence of the* Almanack *lies in its prognostications for the year ahead.*